Stop Surviving and Start Thriving

Stop Surviving and Start Thriving

LEARN HOW TO KICK FEAR AND DOUBT TO THE CURB, MAKE FRIENDS WITH UNCERTAINTY AND RECLAIM YOUR DESTINY

Julie Carr

ISBN-13: 9780988878129
ISBN-10: 0988878127

This book is dedicated to Madison, Noah and Zoe.
May you always find the courage to step with boldness into your
God-gifted destiny.
Always remembering that this destiny is yours to claim with
courage and intention.
For it has been yours before there was time and space.
I love you and fiercely believe in you.

Table of Contents

INTRODUCTION

Open Water. Not what I expected!

> "Go confidently in the direction of your
> dreams! Live the life you have imagined."
> — HENRY DAVID THOREAU

Have you ever placed yourself in a situation you felt you were completely unable to handle? I mean seriously unable to handle. Not the kind where you can turn your blinker on and do a U turn and redirect. I am talking about the kind of situation where you think in your head, "Holy cow what have I done?"

That is exactly where I found myself.

It was 7:30 am in the middle of June. There I was, in the middle of the lake, unable to move and the water was so cold, my arms felt like lead. I was terrified. I couldn't breathe. The only sound I could hear and feel was my heart beating. The voices in my head and sheer panic completely overwhelmed me. It was at that moment when I thought to myself, "What have you gotten yourself into?" I was paralyzed with indecision. What am I going to do? It was as if all time stopped and waited for my decision. The harsh reality was, I had no choice. I had to continue to swim. To move forward with all the strength I had in me and I was a life or death situation.

Or was it?

Slowly, the more rational voices in my head began to prevail. "Get ahold of yourself. Calm down, for goodness sakes. It's going to be fine. You are not going to die. I repeat, you are not going to die."

At that point, I began to control my breathing. I closed my eyes and centered myself. As I did the memory of a promise I had made to myself six months prior filled the portal of my frontal cortex. Slowly, I began to find strength and a surge of momentum. I began to move forward. I felt myself making progress. I put one arm in front of the other, and my legs moving in synchronous motion. As I did so I became aware of the sounds around me. They were the sounds of cheering, people swimming and taking in breaths of air as they moved forward with great might. Water splashed all around me from the hundreds of other swimmers competing. I was still terrified and afraid that I could not do this. That I was unable keep up with the other athletes and that maybe, just maybe, I would fail or even worse, drown.

Six months prior to this terrifying event, I had decided to attempt a triathlon. I am an athlete. I always have been. Running is my sport. I had three grueling marathons under my belt. I enjoy setting athletic goals, ones that seems unattainable, and achieving it. It brings me an enormous amount of satisfaction. But this time was different. This time I was frightened. This time I was completely outside of my comfort zone. And I was not enjoying it. The high that I normally get from the completeness strangely eluded me and left me with fear and her evil twin, doubt, in the lead role.

Prior to finding myself shoved tight in a very uncomfortable wet suit, I did not know how to swim. Oh yes, I could doggie paddle with the best of them. I could tread water for a lengthy five minutes on a good day. Yet, this type of competitive swimming required skill, confidence and more importantly, technique. All three of which I lacked. Prior to the race I had done some training in the high school pool. Let me emphasize, some training. Much of my sporadic behavior may have had to do with the fact that the pool hours were from 6 am until 7:30 am. Typically, I am having my morning coffee and reading my bible at 7 am in a warm robe and furry slippers. Driving to the pool, let alone getting in the freezing cold water seemed like genius the night before, but not so attractive the next morning. Regretfully, I missed most days telling myself that my natural athletic skills will provide the foundation for not only finishing the race, but placing in the top 10%.

In retrospect, I realize that lack of preparation is a large reason why most of us feel ill prepared to face goals and obstacles in life that we may otherwise face with confidence. My particular lack of commitment and dedication left me unprepared for what I was about to face. Not only did I feel unprepared physically, but emotionally as well. Commitment, focus and dedication are keys in your ability to confidently take steps toward your dreams. Stepping outside of your comfort zone can be a fearful experience. Reaching towards uncertainty is better attempted if you are focused, dedicated to a goal, and committed to seeing it through; No matter what.

I did not drown that cold morning in June. I finished the race and placed sixth in my age group. Not bad for a rookie. What if I would have trained more? What if I would have dedicated my swim time and received some coaching? Watched YouTube videos on proper technique? What if I would have thrown myself in, 100%? What if? Could I have placed first in my age group, overall? I placed first in my age group in the run. Yet running is my strongest event. I am a natural runner. I love it. Hence, I do it all the time. Running required less discipline and dedication.

I have since gone on to compete in a multitude of triathlons. I am happy to report that I continue to place in the top three of my age group with an occasional first place finish. Not because I am lucky or I can run faster than most of the participants. It is because I "got it". I realized that if I deeply desire something, I mean really, really want something, I need to commit wholeheartedly and take massive action towards its attainment.

You may be asking yourself, "What does this have to do with me, uncertainty and my destiny?" If you and I were having coffee together, discussing this book, I would tell you it has everything to do with your true destiny. To truly live the life of thriving and not just surviving you need to be willing to step outside of all that you perceive is comfortable and certain. It is then you begin to see small victories. These small victories fuel your confidence and silence your fear and doubt. When the fear and doubt are silenced, you are able to see clearly all that you are capable of doing, being, and becoming. When you begin to believe that what you want is not only possible, but worth the fight, it is then that you can take steps outside of your comfort zone and embrace the land of uncertainty with confidence

I wrote this book for you. I wrote this book for everyone who is living a life with a low grade fever of dissatisfaction. You know deep in your soul that life is more than paying bills, taking care of kids, doing laundry, watching your favorite TV shows, going to bed, waking up and doing it all over again. You long for more. You yearn for the knowledge in your soul that you are living the life you were created to live. Living the *Why* of why you exist. I am here to tell you, there is more. You can have more. You can know deep in your heart that you are living your life fully alive and on purpose. You can live a life where you thrive on a daily basis and not simply surviving the day to day mundaneness of it all. I am living proof that it can be done and I am going to show you how. Life is not perfect. You will make mistakes. We all do. It is part of learning and growing. If you never made a mistake you could never learn how to do something better, more efficient, more fun, and more thrilling. Mistakes teach us what not to do. That is if you heed their warning labels. Albert Einstein reminds us that the definition of insanity is doing the same thing over and over expecting a different result. Stepping outside the boundaries of what you believe is certain (also known as the comfort zone) allows you to make mistakes. The inside of a comfort zone is a dangerous place giving you the allure that all is well. Well, I am here to tell you that is a lie. The biggest lie you could ever believe and one that could cost you a lifetime of wasted opportunities, experiences, relationships, agony and life altering moments. So what are you going to do? Do you want to play it safe? Or, do you want to play it risky and lose the comfort zone and step into uncertainty?

CHAPTER 1

Identifying the "Comfort Zone" and My Story

> "Each of us must confront our own fears, must come
> face to face with them. How we handle our fears will
> determine where we go with the rest of our lives. To
> experience adventure or to be limited by the fear of it."
> —JUDY BLUME

In the spring of 1985 I had big hair, blue eye shadow, matching blue mascara, Calvin Kline Jean sand a high school diploma. That year was the beginning of my life. A life full of opportunities. I was prepared for the world and ready to seize the American Dream. The problem, however, was that I had no idea what I wanted to do or become. I had a vague idea, but nothing with directional purpose. My parents, both wonderful, hard-working people who loved and cared for me deeply, also had no idea how to lead me. Neither of my parents had gone to college after high school. Both my parents held very traditional roles. My Mom was a homemaker and stay-at-home Mom during the time. My Father owned and operated a small Heating and Cooling business where we lived in a small town in Northern Michigan. I was older by ten years than my one sibling, Samuel. I had no clue what to do. I decided to enroll at a University 45 minutes south of where I grew up. The reason behind my choice? All of my friends would be attending the same University. I fumbled through the application phase, enrolled for classes, picked my dorm and off I went. No clue what I was doing and no direction.

Up until this point life had been relatively easy for me. I was popular, had lots of friends, smart, athletic and was a wildly extroverted personality. Moving away from all I knew in our small Northern Michigan town proved to be both challenging and uncomfortable. The uneasy feelings of discomfort propelled me to seek the zone: the comfort zone. Unaware at the time of what was transpiring, I followed what I knew best and whatever caused me the least amount of emotional unrest. Sound familiar? The human race is inclined to be creatures of habit. There is comfort in the habitual, the sameness of routine.

Time to Choose

Universities require that you choose a major area of study. I mean really? Did I have to commit? Or could I just take random classes for the next four years slap a diploma in my hand? Apparently, it does not work that way. Much to my chagrin, I was forced to choose an area of study that would launch me into the American Dream. Too many choices made this inane process difficult for me. Part of me wanted to lay them all out, with the exception of "High School Math Teacher" and throw a dart and see where my future would go. My Academic Advisor felt that was not an option and suggested I choose something that interested me. After some 10 minutes of intense strategizing in my mind, I decided I wanted to be an Athletic Trainer and work for a professional sports team. In my mind it was a perfect match. I loved sports and competition. I am really good at sports. I am intensely competitive. That was a no brainer. American dream here I come. In the spring of 1986, I declared loud and clear with a false sense of confidence that my chosen major was, Sports Medicine. The monkey of pressure to choose was off my back. The next step was to learn what classes were required to take in order to accomplish this feat. And, this all had to be accomplished with a four year time period.

"Who picked the four year rule?" I asked.

Her response, "Because that is how many classes you need to take and that is how long it will take you."

I just stared at her, and thought to myself silent, "You so did not answer my question." We sat in silence for several awkward moments as if she were thinking to herself, "Silly Freshman. It will take her awhile but she'll get it."

I wanted to press on, getting into the American Dream. I thought the whole four year rule ludicrous. I mean why couldn't I do this in say, two years? What possible benefit would there be in wasting my time. After debating with myself, I chose to remain silent. This conversation would take me down Frustration Avenue; a nasty detour out of my comfort zone.

I left her office with a list of classes in hand. On the way back to my dorm room I felt a sense of unease growing. My class list included classes such as, Chemistry, Physics, Math, Physiology and Anatomy. That was all fine and good if I were one of the smart kids. I had labeled myself as socially smart but not necessarily academically smart. I had gotten by in high school Science and Math, true, but I felt absolutely no enjoyment out of the process. Science and Math were necessary evils for that diploma, and my passport stamped to get out of Dodge. Not something I felt a sense of intrigue about or the drive to solve scientific problems and cure world hunger. Nonetheless, I enrolled for the fall semester of my freshman year heavy in Math and Science.

Two weeks into the semester it hit me. My Physics teacher was speaking Latin, or some other foreign language I did not understand. Chemistry was not going any better. I botched my first lab assignment by grabbing the wrong chemicals. When my group discovered what I had done and because of it the whole group would receive a failing grade, I was sure that I just may be voted off the island only two weeks into the semester. Unlike Dale Carnegie, I was not winning friends nor influencing people in my Chemistry lab. Ignoring the nagging feeling in the pit of my gut that something was not right, I soldiered on. What choice did I have? I was young, totally clueless and learning the ropes as I went.

Fast forward to the four years my Advisor prophesied would come. The day I would be liberated, trained and ready to embark on the American Dream. Within those four years I had changed majors four times. Exactly how I pulled that off remains a mystery to this day. My Bachelor's Degree in Applied Arts tells me I am an expert in Public Health Education with a minor expertise in Family Life and Human Sexuality. What I was to do with that exactly remained a little foggy. What I did know was completed all my coursework with at least a C average, my tuition was paid-up, I had made some really cool friends and had fun times.

I can't say that I immediately went on to become an iconic figure in the world of public health. I did, however decide to enroll in graduate school. I was unemployed, living with my parents, lacked a clear career direction, and it sounded like fun. That was the impetus behind the epic decision to attend graduate school and become a master in my field. Doesn't sound very compelling, I know. Because I was unemployed, I lacked funds to survive let alone attend another two years of school at an incredibly hiked up tuition rate. I decided to apply for a graduate teaching assistantship. I had nothing to lose and even fewer options

Much to my amazement I was selected out of 300 other applicants. Beginning late August I would sign up for classes, meet my two mentors and learn what role I would be playing over the next four semesters. At this point I had no clue what a graduate teaching assistant actually did. I assumed I would do some teaching. It was after all part of the job title. Possibly, grade papers, prepare for lectures, or other mundane tasks. I could do that. My area of study was still in the Health Education sector. When all was said and done I would receive a Master of Arts in Health Education. In a Master's program, a minor is not required. I assumed that when you are busy mastering something you would not have time to minor as well. I got that and it made perfect sense to me.

My mentors, two tenured University Professors, quickly became very dear to me and I considered them both role models and the reason for much of my passion to this day. My favorite was Dr. Johnson. He was in his early 60's, stood 6' 3" and possessed a gentle and mild personality that always welcomed students into his office warmly. I will never forget a story he shared with me one day. It left a lasting impression and I use this story for my clients and in workshops whenever I am teaching on perseverance.

Dr. Johnson, a much respected Professor in the Health Sciences Department was bright, articulate and very intelligent. His demeanor exuded confidence. Looking back, I truly believe that is why so many students and his close colleagues were drawn to him. However, it wasn't always that way. While sitting in his office one warm September afternoon going over goals and objectives for a course I was responsible for teaching. As a young boy in junior high he struggled academically. He was a slow reader and had difficulty expressing his thoughts on paper. In his words, "I was a poor student." Today he might been diagnosed with a learning challenge. Many years ago such challenges remained undiagnosed and too often ignored. As a result countless children suffered through years of academic frustration.

I looked at him in amazement. "You really had a hard time reading and even writing? I find that hard to believe because of where you are today. As a University Professor, so much of what you do is research and publishing new work."

He nodded his head and smiled. "Yes, I know. I amaze myself sometimes," he chuckled, looking away as if being taken back to a time in history.

"You know, my 8th grade English teacher told me one day that I should just accept the fact that I will never amount to anything more than a low paying job where I don't have to think much. She told me to pump gas or do basic janitorial work. With my limited ability and skill set that is all I will ever be capable of."

We sat in silence for a moment. It was very clear that the memory was still painful and very real in his mind. I didn't know what to say. I sat there in the moment with him. Then as quickly as it came, it went. He shook his head and smiled, "Boy I'm glad I didn't believe her."

I smiled back, "Yeah, me too."

In that moment, my life was changed. I realized suddenly that I had been privileged to be part of a memory, journeying back to a significant moment that shaped this man's life. It was the kind of moment that changes your life and all the decisions after that and the ones that take you down a different path.

You are free to choose. We are all free to choose. He chose to believe that what his 8th Grade English teacher predicted about him was wrong. He was capable of becoming and doing more. Had he not, we never would have had that conversation and you would not be reading this now. What you choose to believe, or not believe has the power to shape the rest of your life. Choose wisely and *choose with intention*. Never rely on your comfort zone to steer the ship. One of my favorite quotes is by Tony Robbins, "It is in the moment of decision that your destiny is shaped." That was true for Dr. Johnson and it can be true for you and me as well. It is not necessarily in the moments, hours, days or weeks that pass afterwards. It is in the very moment we decide to believe or not to believe.

It is that very moment that we experience a paradigm shift. It is that moment when thoughts change and you begin to entertain the possibilities of a different kind of future. A future beyond what you believed possible. Do not settle for what someone else tells you is the definition of your personal destiny. It is in these moments you tune into that still small voice in your soul that whispers, "You are created for purpose." It is this purpose that we all crave. You and I are not here by accident. Each one of us has a deep calling and meaning for existence than is visible on the surface. It is only when we quiet our minds and seek solitude that we are able to discover what is our deeper calling and purpose. The unfortunate reality is that so many individuals fill their time, minds and day with mindless activities that silence the voice that has all the answers to the questions we ask.

The next two years of graduate school turned out to be two of the best years of my life. Not the easiest, but the best. As a Teaching Assistant, I did just that, I taught. I was responsible for teaching five sections of an undergraduate teaching course under the directorship of my two mentors. The entire experience terrified me. Unfortunately, the fear rarely subsided. There were moments that I would prepare for class, walk in and feel the sweat running down my back as I stood in front of 25 college freshman, some bigger, taller and much stronger than me. I was responsible for the creation of course content in alignment with the goals and objectives set forth as well as the evaluation metrics to measure student success. I literally had no clue what I was doing. I felt as if every time I walked in front of that class I faked every moment. I was terrified that one day my students would see through my fear and call me out as a phony. That lasted for 16 grueling weeks. Yet, each week I pressed on. I continued because it was something I had to do. It was a subtle voice in my soul. The voice that tells you, "You must continue." And not necessarily because I felt forced. I felt a sense of urgency that this is what I must do, regardless of the fear and those pesky doubts that filled my mind daily.

Finally, the end of the first semester came to a close. I was wrapping up my own courses as well as the ones I was teaching. It was a busy time. The holidays were right around the corner and I was eager to be home to celebrate Christmas with my family. It was the Friday before everyone left for break, and campus was a dead zone. I was sitting in the office I shared with five other graduate students, wrapping up final details when I heard a knock at the door. I looked up, somewhat startled, because I was deep in thought and anxious to finish.

"Hey! Got a few minutes?" It was Dr. Palmer, the Dean of the Health Science Department. The question was obviously rhetorical. As if I would say, "No, I am really busy. Please, return another time that is most convenient for me." I chose instead to reply, "Yes, of course. Come on in." A much better response as compared to the one I had conjured up in my head. He sat down across from my desk with a manila folder. He was dressed casually, heading out for the holiday as well.

"I wanted to catch you before you left for break. I didn't want this to wait until you returned in January", he said, making reference to the folder. At that moment my heart sank. I was transported back to kindergarten, standing in front of my teacher, Miss Smith asking my why on earth I would push Billy headfirst into the cabinets while we were both playing in the classroom boat? My response to Miss Smith, "Because I felt like it." The look on her face told me that was not the answer she was searching for. It was the same feeling now.

Oblivious to my screaming fear he went on to say, "You know we compiled the student evaluations. Sarah just finished today as a matter of fact." Keep in mind, this is way before Google. Any compiling that was done was done by hand. Each student's response was carefully recorded by the Department Secretary. So, the fact that Dr. Palmer was in my office on a Friday before break scared me to death.

"I wanted to share some of the student responses with you personally." Seriously dude! You are going to do this to me before I leave? That is cruel and unusual. Don't I have some type of constitutional rights or something? Fifth Amendment? No wait that is the one where I don't have to talk. I tucked that back in my mind. I may need to use that later.

"It appears, you are one of the best graduate teaching students we have ever had. Your evaluations were outstanding. One student wrote that if it weren't for you he would have dropped out of college. Another stated, she learned more in your class than she had from all her others. The staff here is pretty impressed. I figured you might want to know that before you leave." He smiled, handed me the envelope and got up to leave.

"You can keep these. We have the originals. Get some rest over the Christmas break, enjoy your family and we will see you after the New Year." Silently, I reached for the evaluations and smiled at him. The smile was in complete relief. Apparently, I was not in trouble.

After he had left, I just sat there, amazed. I wasn't so much surprised at the evaluations. I was honored by the kind words of my students. What astonished me was the fear that had consumed for 16 grueling weeks. All of the doubt that encompassed my days was a lie. When you think about it, what was I fearful and what exactly did I doubt. Was it my abilities as an instructor? Did I want my students to like me more than I wanted them to learn academic concepts? I didn't really know. I spent the entire Christmas break thinking about it. That was more than 25 years ago and I am still thinking about it today. So much of life is a mystery. It is a "figure it out" as you go type of thing. I don't have all the answers. But, I do know this; going to graduate school was scary. I did it because I believed I had no other options. That is not true. When you believe you have no options, then you do not.

Henry Ford said it best, "There are two types of men. Those that think they can and those that think they can't. They are both right."

If you believe you have options, you have many. It really comes down to a matter of what you believe to be true. Because I am a Christian, I believe that God orders my steps. He takes us all on a divine journey. It is a journey that ultimately will bring us to His plan and purpose for creating us. However, we do have a choice to act a certain way and to embrace what we believe to be our destiny. Fear will lie to you. It will tell you to stay safe. It will use subtle cues to keep you locked in your comfort zone. The reality is, there is no such thing as a comfort zone or safe zone. It is something we make up in our minds to keep the proverbial monsters at bay.

All Comfort is Not Created Equal

Our family loves dogs. We have three. Lisa; a pit bull with a bark is much more ferocious than her bite. Jewel is a 17 year old well-traveled mix of miniature wiener dog and boxer who has been to Key West with us on three separate occasions. Our latest addition is Spike, a pug we rescued and absolutely adore. Pugs are known to be fearless and tenacious. And for the most part he is fearless. However, there are moments when he is paralyzed by indecision. My husband refers to it as being, *locked up*. There he sits in the middle of our backyard motionless, staring at me as I call to him. My pleas become louder and more urgent for him to come inside. It does not matter. When Spike is in lock-mode, you may as well close the door and flick on the TV for your favorite half hour sitcom. Spike is not moving.

How many times do we get *locked up* in a situation, a comment that someone said, or something that failed to go the way we planned. We get into lock-mode, ignoring the support of the ones around us who could help. Paralyzed from taking the step that just might bring us closer to the destiny that is our birthright. Comparing my pug Spike to you is harsh I realize, but you get the message. It is far too easy to get *locked up*, unable to see the opportunities surrounding us. Those opportunities are waiting to be grabbed. Instead, we become immobilized with fear, doubt and the "what if's" syndrome. Be bold enough to ask the, "What if's" and brave enough to face the answer. The "What if" questions spin in our heads like a tit-a-whirl, never stopping and making us nauseous. If not kept in check, we are get consumed with doubt. Doubt leads to fear. Fear leads to paralysis. What if, when you asked that question, while facing the unknown, you were able to say with a sense of confidence, "It may be difficult, but I can handle the worst "what if", if that is what it comes down to?" By doing this, we dismantle the fear, leaving it powerless to take up residence in our thought life.

One of the most powerful stories on courage, strength and stepping outside of your comfort zone in the Bible takes place in the Book of Joshua and it involves Joshua, himself. Let me back up. Moses was the first leader of the Israelites, taking them out of Egypt where they had been slaves for over 400 years. During that 400 year time period their numbers had grown; numbering in the millions. Getting millions Israelites out of Egypt was no easy task. It proved to be even more difficult when they moved out of Egypt and into the wilderness before crossing into the land that God had promised to them. Egypt represented slavery and bondage. Day after day, week after week, month after month and year after year.

Pause here for a moment and think of your life. You may not be thinking your situation compares to the hardships that the Israelites faced. Yet, in many ways it might. Is your bondage to fear and doubt about your future? Perhaps you are kept in slavery by uncertainty, worry and anxiety. Not knowing when, where or how to make a move that will take you into your divine destiny has crippled you into lock-mode. You may be more like the Israelites than you think.

Fast forward forty years. Forty years of walking in the wilderness completely dependent on God for all of their needs. The whole time complaining of how awful it was, even preferring Egypt to their new freedom. So let me get this straight. Moses led millions of God's chosen people out of slavery to freedom but they wanted to go back into slavery.

Why do so many of us go back into slavery? Let me break it down into more modern terms. Our slavery can be a job or career we despise, a dysfunctional relationship, negative thought patterns, a complaining mouth or even worse, addiction. These are examples of modern slavery. We return over and over again to the familiar, because it is what we know. It is our comfort zone. It may not be "comfortable", but it is familiar. Breaking free from slavery is a difficult journey that takes great amounts of strength, courage and intention. Intention is defined as something to be aimed at or a plan. No amount of strength or courage will carry you to your destiny without a strategy. Intention is needed when the journey become difficult to be referenced and revisited when fear and doubt cloud our judgement.

After Moses died, Joshua became the leader. As a mighty warrior, he was brave, courageous physically and mentally strong. No one messed with Joshua. Which, is why I love that in the first chapter of Joshua, God tells him three times to be strong and courageous; to not be afraid. Why would God say that to such a mighty warrior? He told Joshua that because God knows that in our human frailty we experience fear. If fear is left unchecked in our subconscious mind it gives birth to doubt. Doubt leads to worry and worry keeps us from attempting to step outside of our comfort zones. The only way to get to your Promised Land is to step outside of your comfort zone. The only way. Let me remind you of how courageous you can be.

"Have I not commanded you? Be strong and courageous. Do not be afraid; do not be discouraged, for the LORD your God will be with you wherever you go." (Joshua 1:9, NIV)

Programmed to Conform

We have been programed to conform. It starts early. We are conditioned to follow the rules and do what you believe is the best way to walk the path of least resistance. It is engrained deeply within our culture. Unfortunately, by adhering to this way of thinking you not only miss out on some of the greatest opportunities of your life but you just may get to the end and realize it was all a lie. In his book *Start* (2013) Jon Acuff presents a compelling argument for living your dream and purpose in life. He tells his readers to start whatever it is you believe your dream to be. Acuff states that within each one of us is a unique calling and a gift that we are destined to live. Do not wait for someday because someday may never come or, tragically, you may wake up and someday may have come and gone. In one chapter he tells the story of a conversation he had with an elderly woman he met on a plane. The two of them sat next to each other and naturally struck up a conversation. She asked what he did as a profession and he explained that he was an author and speaker and shared his latest book.

After sometime of silence she leaned over and whispered, "What if it's too late and you realize you missed your dream?"

Don't miss your opportunity because you are consuming your time and energy staying within your perceived comfort zone. Life is not meant to be easy. Getting what you want is not easy. If it were, everyone would be doing it and you would hear less complaining from those sorry souls who make excuses as to why they do not have what their hearts truly desire. In order to get the desires of your heart, you need to be willing to risk being uncomfortable with uncertainty.

What I learned from my graduate school experience was even though I was full of fear, doubting that I could pull it off, I proceeded anyway. Even afraid, I just did it. Was it comfortable? Not in the least. I lived in that place outside of my comfort zone for a long period of time, not knowing where I would end up. When I refer to "knowing", it is a sense of deep knowing in your very soul. Not the kind that someone tells you about or that you read in a textbook. It is the type of knowing only found within. It cannot be learned, it can only be listened to. Interestingly, the word "vocation" comes from the Latin root, "vocare", meaning, inner knowing or inner calling. In other words, what are you called to do? Who are you called to be? Not something you put on, it is something you discover and identify.

Many, choose not to listen. They hear the voice. They recognize it with a vague sense of uncertainty. They acknowledge that it may be in their best interest to heed to the calling of the voice. The knowing however does not present itself with an instruction manual. Therein lies the complication for many people. You know the type, perhaps you are one of them, who have a life plan down to the very nanosecond. There is nothing wrong with planning. Planning has its place. The problem becomes when the plan becomes uncomfortable.

I did not know all the details of the plan. I had an idea, a vague inkling of where I needed to go. From there, the choice was mine. Do I follow the knowing and possibly risk feeling afraid? Or, do I ignore the knowing and do what is safe and gives me the illusion of security and safety, the ever popular comfort zone. I chose to follow the knowing that led me down an unlit path. No script. No final destination with a big blinking arrow that screams, "You have arrived!" I just kept trudging along feeling the fear every day. I placed a John Wayne quote on my bathroom mirror to remind me:

"Courage is being scared to death, but saddling up anyway." Wise words.

I knew deep in my soul that life could be more than what I could see with my eyes. I wanted more. I wanted all that I was created to be. That required tuning in to my vision. Tuning into your vision is scary and at times unclear. It requires a certain level of trust. Not trust in outside circumstances, but the kind that is between you and yourself. I did not know how things were going to work out, or where. I did not know what exactly it would look like. I just knew that I couldn't stop. And I did not.

Life doesn't suddenly change for you overnight. You will not reach your destination with a single bound over a tall building, like Superman. It takes daily work and daily commitment. It is the type of commitment which links to a purpose and reason bigger than you may be privy to at this point. Trust the knowing. Trust that you will make it out. You will be able to get to the other side. What is the alternative? The comfort zone. I am here to tell you a great big secret. Are you ready? The comfort zone is a big fat lie. Now we can move on.

Take Action

1. **Embrace discontent and emotional unrest.**
   We feel as if any type of activity or challenge that causes us emotional unrest is a bad thing. Review it. See if this thing is going to

move you toward your goal or away from your goal. All emotional unrest is not created equal. Just because something feels uncomfortable does not mean it is bad for you. It may mean just the opposite. It may be very thing you need to embrace. Write down the areas of your life that you are feeling a type of discontent or an emotional unrest. You may want to separate them into professional and personal. For example, are you feeling a discontent in your current job? Do you feel as if you are not being challenged? Or, maybe you are not using your skills and natural talents to the fullest in the current position you are in? Are you waiting for someday to leave and find something better? *Someday is today.* Begin today to move outside of your comfort zone. Staying in a job that is paying the bills and keeping you in a state of emotional numbness is not good. It may feel comfortable--now. Fast forward ten years and you will most likely be in the same place you are now; but older with fewer options and less enthusiasm for making a change. Evaluate you level of discontent. If you feel in your heart you need to make a change, even a minor one, do it now. Take that first step outside of your comfort zone. It does not have to be a monumental one. Remember the quote by Lao-tzu, the Chinese Philosopher, "The journey of a thousand miles begins with a single step.

_____

_____

_____

_____

_____

_____

2. **Make an inventory of what you really, really want.**
   This is an incredibly useful exercise. One that will open up your mind to the possibilities of having an outstanding life. Too often we become lulled into believing that what we really want is not possible; that in order to live the good life, you need to take the more secure route. The reality is there is no secure route. There is no safe zone. The most effective way to create a safe zone for yourself is to create life on your terms. That begins with discovering what it is

you really want. When I work with clients or teach workshops I so often hear what people do not want. I hear things like, "Well, I sure don't want to do that job again!" or "I don't want to end up broke having to depend on my kids to take care of me." Rarely do I hear people say what they truly desire and voice it out loud on a daily basis. What we focus on grows and becomes our reality. Rather than focus on what you don't want, focus on what you do want. I am not referring to the things you think people want to hear or what you believe sounds good in front of others. I am referring to what you truly desire. The Psalmist tells us to,

> *Delight yourself also in the Lord, and He will give you the desires and secret petitions of your heart* (37:4, NIV).

For this discussion, focus on the latter portion of the verse. God plants His desires for your heart; meaning you have them in your heart already. The challenge is to identify your desires in order to begin to focus on those desires and begin to devise a plan and strategy to achieve them. Spend some time alone in quiet meditation. Ask God to reveal your true desires. Write them down and look at them daily. You will be amazed at the progress you will make in the days, weeks, months and years ahead towards goals and aspirations that are in true alignment with your soul.

_____

_____

_____

_____

_____

_____

3. **Listen to the voice of the knowing.**
   In each one of us is placed the voice of what I call, *the knowing.* It is the still, soft voice that gives heed to warnings of not only impending danger, but of opportunity as well. We know that danger brings feelings of fear. But, what we may not realize is that opportunity may come clothed in the same feeling. Just because it

does, does not mean you should stop and not proceed. What you need to do is stop and evaluate. Evaluate based on your own intuition and the still small voice in your heart. When we are young we hear the voice and it is loud and clear. It is not uncomfortable for us to act on that voice. Somewhere from birth to where you are now, you may have turned down the volume on that voice. It may have come at inopportune times, telling you to act on an opportunity or release yourself from a person or even a job that was no longer serving your life purpose. When that happens, stress shows up as well, urging you to make a choice. Now. And you begin to understand that choosing also involves risk. You risk losing a friend, a supposedly secure situation for the unknown, or losing your definition of normal. The more we turn down the voice to serve us in a moment of convenience, the less likely we are to hear or recognize the voice.

Your inner voice, the part of you seeking to guide, becomes quieter and less clear, like an echo that fades into the wind. And then, one day we wake up and realize it has left. Do not let that happen. Even in moments of discomfort, stop and evaluate, then act. Not according to what you believe to be right for the immediate security, but for the long run. For your future. You only have one life. There are no do-overs. God has gifted you with a very unique set of talents and gifts. Use them wisely and with abandon.

That still small voice in your heart not only prompts you towards your deepest desires and goals, but serves as a warning signal as well. You know that voice well.

It's the one that quietly whispers in times of decision, "I really don't think this is a good idea. Stay away from this situation/person/venture." In those moments it is of utmost important that you stop and take time to evaluate the situation. Ask yourself if this move towards an idea, job, business venture or possible new friendship is in true alignment with your life purpose and long term goals. If not, you may need to walk away. You may even need to walk away from certain relationships that no longer serve you. I certainly do not mean that in an egotistical way. Nor am I insinuating you walk away from a friendship or relationship in a cruel way. What I am suggesting is that

you inventory your life. Taking stock of what is filling your valuable
time. Are they things or people that uplift you or are they things that
trap you at a level much lower than your true capabilities. Take some
time to do a thorough and honest evaluation of the things and people
in your life. Is there anything or anyone that needs to be moved out?

_____

_____

_____

_____

_____

_____

4. **Believe that what you truly seek is possible.** It really does begin
   with belief. What you decide in your mind to believe is what your
   brain will seek to find. Decide that you are capable and worthy
   of more than where you are now. Know that you were created for
   purpose with a certain type of talent that is uniquely yours gifted
   to you by the Creator of the Universe.

   Write down in a personal notebook what you believe, or want
   to believe is possible for your life. It can be one sentence if that
   is where you need to begin. The key is to begin and that may be
   your very first step outside of your comfort zone. Don't play small
   either. Write down what you want to believe is possible. Be careful
   to not allow your current circumstances to restrict or dictate what
   you believe is the plan and possibility for your future. Part of moving outside of a comfort zone is beginning with a vision of what
   we believe to be possible for our lives. I like to use the example of
   a GPS system that so many of us use to navigate while driving to a
   new destination. When the GPS fails, very rarely, is it because there
   is a default in the system. The GPS typically fails to take me to my
   destination if I have put in the wrong coordinates. I cannot order
   my GPS system, to take me to a destination if I have no clear idea
   of the destination myself. This is similar to our lives. If you do not
   have a destination in mind, how will you get there? You may be
   thinking, "I really don't know what I want." If I were sitting next
   to you I would say, "Yes you do. You just have not taken the time

to carefully *and with purpose* figure that out." We all know what we truly want. The reality in many cases is that we are fearful that if we admit it and even dare speak it, what if it never works out? What if I dream this really cool dream and I don't get it? Then what? So rather than dream and hope and plan we decide staying in the familiar places of our so-called comfortable lives is easier than facing possible disappointment. I know I am right because I have been there.

It was only when I decided to move past that, taking some calculated, and some not so calculated, steps away from that mindset did I begin to open my mind to the belief that I could have more and be more. That is a powerful and empowering thought. Write down what you want to believe is possible for your life. Not what you see right now in your current circumstances, but what you want to see happen in your life. It could be in your career, in your marriage, as a parent, in your health or finances. Write it down with the belief that it is possible.

In the book of Matthew chapter 25 Jesus tells his disciples the parable of the talents. If you are unfamiliar, let me do a quick overview. Three servants each received what the Bible refers to as a talent from their master. The word talent in this context is referring to a gift given to each one of us. For purposes of this book, the gift is referring to a unique skill and strength that is uniquely yours, gifted by God. The parable goes on to tell that one of the servants, the one with the most talents, doubled his investment by not hiding the talents but looking for ways to increase what he already had. This servant went out, stepped out of his comfort zone, took some calculated risks and doubled his resources. The second servant did a similar thing. Although he had fewer talents, he nevertheless took the risk to invest what he had and doubled them. The last servant who had received one talent acted out of fear and hid the one talent in the ground. . Rather than use his talent creatively, and yes maybe a little risky, he decided to bury it in the ground. By doing this he did in fact keep what he had, but that was it. Upon the master's return, each servant came to report what they had done. The first two servants reported that they had used their talents to the fullest and in return they were able to double their investment. The master was very pleased. The last servant was a different story. When he approached the master he told him with a smile, he still had the talent. Out of fear this servant played it safe. He hid what little he had. The result; his lack of vision angered the master so that this servant's one talent was taken from him and given to those who had followed a vision to increase what they had been given.

I love that parable because I believe it is such a great representation of our lives. You have been gifted. How dare you hide your gift from the world and the people that need it the most? There is someone out there who needs what you have to give. By playing it safe, burying your talent and staying within your comfort zone you are actually diminishing the gift that God has given you. When you hide your talents in fear, everyone loses; not just you. You are created for more. You are created to step outside of the zone. The intention was never for you to stay.

_____

_____

_____

_____

_____

_____

CHAPTER 2

The Safety Zone Myth and Other Lies Your Mama Told You

"Inaction breeds doubt and fear. Action breeds confidence
and courage. If you want to conquer fear, do not sit
home and think about it. Go out and get busy."
— DALE CARNEGIE

My husband, Chris, is an artist in the truest sense of the word. The visual picture that most of us get in our heads when we think of the word "artist" is a Picasso or Michael Angelo. Yet, art can be anything that you create to make the world a better place not only for yourself but for others as well. According to Daniel Pink in his book, *A Whole New Mind*, (2005) our culture is moving from an information age to that of a conceptual age. Because we now have access to the internet and information is plentiful with the simple click of a mouse, we are able to move into more right-brained types of activities. These types of activities can bring not only a great deal of personal satisfaction, but income as well. We are able to connect with individuals from all over the world. This is something that could not have been accomplished just a decade ago. The connection of individuals from other states, countries or even continents was only a fantasy then and has now become a reality. This reality has made the possibilities of moving outside of your comfort zone amazingly simple and easily accessible.

When my husband, Chris first entered college in the early 80's he decided to opt for a degree in business. When I asked him why he chose that field his response was quick, "Because I thought I could make a lot of money." This is followed with, "Boy was I off on that assumption." That was more than 30 years ago. Things have changed. Namely, three children, three dogs and a mortgage. Life becomes more complicated and choices are harder to come by the deeper ingrained you become in this thing called life. However, the benefit of experience brings wisdom and a deeper sense of direction along with the ability to decipher what you truly want. Part of knowing what you really want is being able to identify what you are intrinsically gifted at doing. Each one of us is born with a certain gift or strength that is uniquely ours and ours alone. Strength is defined by Webster's Dictionary as, *a strong attribute or inherent asset.*

As a certified Career and Life Coach, I have worked one on one with hundreds of people. Much to my dismay most people struggle with defining their innate gifts. When asked the question, "What are you naturally good at?" I am met with a pause and a look of confusion. Almost as if to say, I really don't get the question, followed by hesitant responses that sound more like labels than gifts and talents. Why do we struggle with defining our talents? If you asked a small child what they are good at or an even better question, "What do you love to do? "A child would not hesitate to respond and you may hear more than you anticipated.

When my niece, Magdalynn, was 6 years old, she told me that she was going to be Judge when she grew up so that she could make rules that are good. Simple and directly to the point. What about you? Do you know what you want to be when you grow up? Being grown up is not necessarily defined by an age. There are many individuals in their 40's, 50's and even 60's who are still deciding what they want to be when they grow up. You can learn more about how to figure out the process out in my workbook, *7 Ways to Discover Your Passion, Live Your Purpose & Take Back Your Life!* © (2014).

Somewhere between birth and adulthood we lose our sense of creativity and wonder for life. We lose what Helen Keller so eloquently envisioned when she said, "Life is either a daring adventure or nothing". She goes on to say, "Security is mostly a superstition. It does not exist in nature, nor do the children of men as a whole experience it. Avoiding danger is no safer in the long run than outright exposure. "

Read that again, especially the part about security being a superstition. What is your definition of security? What would happen if all of that went away? What would you do then? Live in fear and misery the rest of your life? Or, would you seek a new adventure realizing that the reality is that security is something we choose to define. Security is the first cousin of your comfort zone. It is a lie. Redefine it. That is your only hope of survival.

The reason I believe that most of us are unable to define what we are naturally gifted at is because deep down we are afraid. We are afraid that if we identify our gifts, categorically define them, we are then placed in a position that we have to acknowledge the existence of the gift. What do we do then?

For too many of us, it is easier to keep the voice quiet than risk coming face-to-face with our deepest desires, only to realize they may elude us. So, we stay in our comfort zone and pretend that all is well. Filling the void with whatever will satisfy us or quiet the growing discontent that is erupting within our souls. Henry David Thoreau describes well the soul's torment, "Most men lead lives of quiet desperation and go to the grave with their song still in them." Waiting for someday or even worse, when you are supposedly ready, is sinking sand. Don't even get near it. The illusion that "one day" will come and you will be prepared for your journey is a seductive lie from the enemy.

The bible tells us that we have an enemy. And that the enemy is seeking to destroy us.

"The thief comes only to steal and kill and destroy; I have come that they may have life, and have it to the full." (John 10: 10 NIV)

If he can't kill you physically, he will kill your dreams, desires, joy and zest for life that Jesus died to give us. You are created to live a life of fullness. When you and I chase desires and dreams that are not ours to chase or avoid realizing our potential, the enemy has succeeded in destroying our future. Hold on tight, pray, believe and step out. You'll be so glad you did.

Honey! I'm home.

I will never forget the day. It was the middle of September and unseasonably warm. Our oldest daughter, Madison had just started kindergarten. Our two youngest, Noah and Zoe were two and one year respectively.

Life was interesting to say the least. I was primarily a stay-at-home Mom and worked occasional contract positions to bring in extra cash to feed our growing family. Madison had just gotten home from her half day of school and we were in the backyard swinging and playing. I looked at the driveway as my husband, Chris, drove in. I looked at my watch thinking that it was early and very unusual for him to be home at this time. He got out of the car, dressed in his best suit, and headed to the backyard to greet us. I smiled to greet him as I pushed Noah on the swing hearing my son's high pitched voice as the swing went back and forth, "Higher Mama! Higher!" So of course, I pushed him higher. Praying he would hang on and not fall, propelling his two-year-old body into the air like a skilled circus performer.

As Chris got closer, I saw the look on his face. It was a look of stress and concern. "What's wrong? I asked somewhat alarmed, yet trying not to show it.

He looked at me for a moment in silence. Have you ever had someone do that to you? It really stinks. If you are like me, there are a million things going on in your head about the possibilities of the words that will come out in the next few minutes may alter your future forever. And then finally he spoke!

"I quit my job." There. It was out. He just looked at me, waiting for my response.

I was speechless. And that does not happen often. I love my husband. I love him very much. But at this moment I was not feeling the love. I was feeling like slapping him and saying, "Are you crazy, man?"

Instead I responded with, "You did what?"

He stood next to the swing set and began to take off his tie. Our kids totally oblivious to the meaning the situation, were still swinging and squealing with glee. Chris took a deep breath and looked up at the clear, blue sky for a long moment. When his eyes finally met mine he said,

"Jules, I was dying. Every day I go into that office a piece of my soul dies. I just couldn't do it anymore."

That was the beginning of living our lives outside of the comfort zone. It was that moment for my husband when a decision was made. According to Tony Robbins, the change starts when the decision is made in our minds.

Mother May I? Or, did Simon Say I could?

These are the decisions that change the shape and feel of your destiny. You suddenly see a glimpse of a future and realize you need to change course. I wish I could say that it was easy after that. It was extremely difficult. Do I recommend you quit your job? Depends? Each one of us is different and we face circumstances that are unique to our situation. You may be the type of person who needs a complete state change. A state change is when you change directions quickly. The direction could be emotional or physical; like quitting your job. You may need to drastically alter your reality in order to motivate yourself to move forward. Others can do this without drastic measures. You may be the person who prefers a slow and steady pace. Either way, the path is not clear and do not expect it to be. If you expect that once you make a decision all will be well, think again. Be prepared to face challenging situations and that you will experience fear and doubt like you never have before. That is normal. Because you feel these things do not in any way indicate you are doing something wrong. It may very well mean you are doing everything right.

As a culture we tend to not be comfortable with feelings of uncertainty. Mainly because all our lives we have been spoon fed the myth of security and playing it safe. We have been taught ever since we were young children that playing it safe was the best thing we could do. It is embedded in our culture like a dangerous tick. It begins when we are small and enter formal education. We are introduced to the educational culture with twenty-five other little people. Not the same developmentally, but in age. Who made that rule?

In his book, *Free Agent Nation; The Future of Working for Yourself,* (2002) Daniel Pink tells us that it wasn't until the 1920's that it became mandatory to attend school. He refers to it a compulsory mass schooling that was put into place to train our youth to become the *Organization Man.* The *Organization Man* in this context is referred to as the person who is the rule follower, the factory worker and the middle manager with minimal skills and knowledge; just enough to follow the rules and not make any waves. You learned the skill of pleasing your teacher so eventually you can please your boss. In other words, you never create havoc and you remain steadfastly within the security zone. You are to remain quiet, sit in rows, never offer much of your opinion, did as you were told, and life was grand. Or was it?

I am in no way indicating that public education is in some way a bad thing. I was educated in a public school system. I have had the privilege of having known educators who are passionate and brilliant. That isn't the point here. I am in no way debating whether teachers or education are evil or angelic. My argument for the purposes of this book is that at a very young age we are taught and witness many influences that compel us to conform to rules and imposed norms. It is in this process that we lose something. We lose the ability to listen to what our inner voice is telling us for fear of stepping outside of what is considered the culturally acceptable thing to do according to the masses. Some people go their entire lives living according to someone else's rules and direction. At what point do we have the courage to step outside of the imposed norms and stand up for what is rightfully our birthright; to live a life that is in alignment with our natural gifts and talents. It is easy in our culture to stay quiet and not make waves. We learn to sit just outside the sidelines as the observer, as life passes us by.

In an effort to comfort ourselves we say things like, "Someday I will do what I want", "When the kids are grown then I can really live!" "When I have enough money, then I will start that business". Sound familiar? It does to me. I have heard myself say those things. They start out ever so subtly. At first they seem to bring comfort, almost as if you are setting a long term goal. Then, as the years begin to pass that comfort slowly turns into discontent which plants the seed for resentment which if left unattended gives birth to a low grade misery. In her book, *Wake Up And Live,* (1980) Dorthea Brande says that each one of us suffers from the *Will to Fail.* We live our lives so focused on what we cannot do or fearful of the discomfort that great amounts of effort will cost, that we focus on failing rather than succeeding. You may be nodding your head thinking that Dorthea may have bumped her noggin. Think about that concept for a moment. How many times have you gone to such great efforts to avoid pain? This pain could take the shape of a conflict, a difficult conversation, quitting a job you hate, leaving a relationship that is harmful for you, or standing up for something you truly believe in. One of my favorite motivational speakers and teacher, Tony Robbins, says that people are simple. We seek to avoid pain or to gain pleasure. What if your avoidance of pain was simply for the short term and in reality costing you a lifetime of happiness?

I was recently faced with a very difficult situation. I delayed the decision for weeks. I knew that I had to face it, but was reluctant. Deep in my soul, I knew that I needed to leave a collaborative business relationship that was no longer serving me or the purpose for which it was intended. For months, I put off the inevitable, telling myself that maybe I was wrong. Maybe if I held on a little longer it would all work out? I reasoned with my deeper knowing that too many people quit, give up and never see their goals accomplished. It all sounded so good. Or so I thought. Here was the problem; it wasn't true and I knew it. You can lie to yourself all you want, but there will always be a piece of your soul that knows the truth and tries desperately to reveal it to you. For me the reality was, I was avoiding the inevitable because I wanted to avoid the short term pain it would cause. Each time I tried to say it, the words would not come out. I knew it, but had a problem acting on my gut instinct

Is that you? If you answered yes or nodding your head, you and I are in the majority, and Dorthea Brande is right after all. We do seek to fail. Rather than facing the facts and owning up to what needs to be done, we take the easy way out. We avoid the short term pain for the very short term and not very pleasurable relief it will bring us as to put off another day what needs to be done. That my friends is called, living inside your comfort zone. If we are honest with ourselves, we know that by taking action towards what we know deep in our souls to be the right thing, even though painful in the beginning, is the right thing to do. It is that very action that leads us towards the edges of our comfort zone. With enough courage and continued action, we begin to get closer to stepping over the line and into our destiny. It is true. Your destiny is not inside what you perceive to be comfortable. If you play it safe all of your life, you will get to the end and realize what you have done. Do not be that person! Live with boldness and courage. Step outside of what you perceive to be comfortable. Not necessarily all at once. Take small steps each day. The key is consistency. One of my favorite quotes is by Eleanor Roosevelt, "Do something each day that scares you." The onetime First Lady was wise in her counsel. She knew the secret. She knew that in order to get out of life what you desire and were created for you need to go and get it. You need to create the life you want. That creation is often painful, intimidating and required an astonishing amount of commitment.

One particular sermon I recently listened to by the Bishop T.D. Jakes was about commitment. (TD Jakes, Commitment, 2014) He bellows to his congregation the cost of giving up and not committing to what you truly desire. So many poor souls sit on the sidelines day after day, too afraid to really commit. And all because, true and lasting commitment takes work, effort and action in the face of uncertainty. It is when you decide to commit to your destiny that you are able to move towards the edges of your comfort zone. Theodore Roosevelt once said, "Far better is it to dare mighty things, to win glorious triumphs, even though checkered by failure . . . than to rank with those poor spirits who neither enjoy nor suffer much, because they live in a gray twilight that knows not victory nor defeat."

Eventually I did confront the situation. Cowardly, I might add. No, I am not proud took it took as long as it did. However, the situation was confronted nonetheless. Much to my amazement, it turned out better than I had anticipated. The news was well received and all is well. Most importantly, I followed my gut, albeit later than it should have been, but I heard it, listened and acted. The result is a fresh perspective on my future. The low grade fever or discontent began to dissipate when I was true to my soul. I won. My inner voice was heard. And life keeps moving and I keep stepping to the edge of what I perceive to be comfort and uncertainty.

The Aftermath

After the bomb was dropped in the backyard by the swing set, it took Chris six months to find another job. During that time I was blessed with more than enough contract work and great budgeting skills. Our children are growing as I type this page. Our oldest daughter, Madison, who at that time was just starting kindergarten has now just finished her first year as a college freshman. With his new job, my husband was able to focus on a passion he has had all his life. A talent and gift he was born to do. It has taken a great deal of time, discipline, and focus, but with a great big vision and calculated strategy he is transitioning to starting a business he had only dreamed of. Living a life he had only imagined. We are able to see the glimpse of this vision becoming our reality. I smile when I am reminded of a quote by Henry David Thoreau: "Go confidently in the direction of your dreams! Live the life you have imagined and you will meet with success in uncommon hours."

Could this have been possible had Chris not quit his job that September afternoon? No, I don't believe it could. Not for us. I believe it was in stepping outside our perceived security that was the impetus for the direction and the path we are now on.

What about you? What decisions do you need to make to change the direction of your life? How can you step outside of your comfort zone to live the life you have only imagined?

I would by lying to you if I told you that following what you truly desired was easy. It is far from easy and there are many moments of self-doubt. The moments where you and I question ourselves, secretly wanting to default back to the comfort zone. That place that was lukewarm, offering neither the valley nor the mountain top. It is almost as if it is a daily battle. I am reminded of what the Word of God speaks regarding our struggles with conformity;

"For our struggle is not against flesh and blood, but against the rulers, against the authorities, against the powers of this dark world and against the spiritual forces of evil in the heavenly realms." (Ephesians 6:12 NIV)

There are forces against you that want to take all that God planned for you to possess. Hold it firmly. If you have to do battle daily, do battle daily. Mark 11:24 tells us,

For this reason I am telling you, whatever you ask for in prayer, believe (trust and be confident) that it is granted to you, and you will [get it] (NIV).

What caught my attention about this verse is the particular word, desire. After some research, I discovered that the word that the author is referring to in this context means, "Craving enough to sacrifice for". In other words, how bad do you want to live an amazing life that impacts others in a significant way? It truly is the path less traveled. Many will enter the wide gate, but few will enter the narrow.

Just for a little bit?

The decision to marry my husband in 1991 was not only because he was extremely attractive, but because I saw a future in his eyes. I saw a future full of purpose, intention and endless possibilities. If we admit it, we all have grand ideas of how things should be. Our vision will often only include the grand moments of laughter, intimacy and progress. Very rarely do we take into consideration all of the pain we will endure along the journey. Pain that, if used wisely, will shape our character. This pain is the tool that God uses to shape us into His Image in order that we may become the very person we are created to be. I like to refer to it as, *pain with a purpose.*

Like any other marriage, mine has had its ups and downs. There were times that if felt like way more down than up. Cleaving and growing together can be a challenging process. Because neither my husband nor I have been very traditional in our work model, the road has been bumpy, winding, uphill, downhill and every way in between.

Recently, while having lunch together, my husband began telling me about an issue he was having at his day job; a job that he did not particularly enjoy nor from which he garnered a sense of fulfillment. He described to me an ongoing problem that seemed to be nationwide, but more so within the state of Michigan, where we live. After describing the problem, which seemed pretty hopeless, he said, "I actually have a solution to the problem." And from there he went on to describe in vivid detail how he would "solve" the problem and in the process be compensated very well.

"How long have you been thinking of this?" I asked.

"Quite a while." He smiled. "I have a lot of down time and my mind wanders. I like to think of solutions to problems. It's fun for me."

He was right on that. He is a master problem solver in a very politically correct way within the corporate environment. I have witnessed him talk with people who were very angry and were not in any way willing to budge on finding a reasonable solution. After talking with my husband, they melted and were ready to find a way to work peacefully together. I am always amazed at how he does that. Blows my mind.

We sat in silence, both eating our lunch. My mind was racing thinking of all the possibilities if my husband decided to embark on this venture. Finally after what seemed like forever, I blurted out, "Why don't you just do it already? I mean, that would be really cool and in all honesty it would take a lot of pressure off of us financially." I waited for his response.

"Jules, no. I don't want to do that. It is a huge undertaking. That is not where my heart is. It would only be about money. You know I am not about only that. Life is more to me than that."

And with that he got up from the table to put his dishes in the sink to start the second half of the day. On his way back to his office he reached over and kissed my head, "Love you." And he was off. Just like that.

It wasn't over for me. I could feel myself getting angry. I could feel a pain beginning to emerge from the pit of my stomach. A surge of emotions began to engulf my brain, coming directly from the back where my amygdala is located. Our amygdala is an almond shaped gland that is responsible for our emotions; it is essentially our fight or flight response to a particular stimulus. If not brought under control by our frontal cortex, it will run rough shot over our lives causing us to react emotionally rather than cognitively. Potential danger for sure. I knew all of this of course. However, I was choosing to ignore it thank you very much.

"How dare he not take that opportunity?" I reasoned to myself. "How could he be so selfish?" I continued stewing and brewing every negative emotion I could conjure up to pacify my irrational thought process. I admit I let it go far too long. I know better. I know in my head not to let a negative emotion take root. It will inevitably end in destruction. I eventually marched my way to Chris' office. "Hey. I need to talk to you." I said, trying not to sound too angry.

He turned, with a surprised look on his face, "Yea? Ok? About what?" He truly was surprised. He had no idea that he was about to be ambushed.

"I think that by you not taking action on this venture, you are being selfish!" I blurted out. Feeling somewhat childish as I actually heard the thoughts formed as words. I immediately wanted to take them back. I had defied my own 24 hour rule. The 24 hour rule is the one where you wait

24 hours before responding. Typically 24 hours is adequate time to cool down and think rationally.

"What? Are you being serious?" He asked.

"Yes. I am being very serious." I was in too deep now. "We could use the money. I think it is foolish you are not at least looking into this opportunity."

"Jules, do you have any idea how long something like that would take to build. The process it would be to get everything in place. I am in my 50's. I would ultimately be miserable. Is that what you want? Is that more important to you than me staying true to who I am?" He voice was calm and sincere.

I realized at that very moment what I had done. I realized that I let the idea of a temporary solution take the place of a vision that he and I were working towards. My purpose and mission in life is to encourage, inspire and equip individuals to live out loud their God gifted potential and to do that with courage and intention. Here I was, questioning my life partner. Would I have spoken to a client that way? Absolutely not. I would have told my client to dream big. Go for what you really want. Don't stop until you get there. I completely lost sight of the goal; my husband's vision and dream. I knew at that moment, I mean really knew what Henry David Thoreau meant when he said, *"Live the life you have dreamed."* There is no other life. There is no promise of tomorrow. There is only now. I admire and respect my husband for staying true to what he believes to be his passion and vision. It takes strength and courage in a world that screams at him as a man, a husband, father and leader to conform to societal norms. I had different lenses that day. I looked at the world a little differently. I dug my heels in deeply into my own beliefs and values about how life should be and how each of us should live our own individual lives and mission.

How often we try so desperately to avoid the pain of the here and now through short term fixes. We stay at the job that is killing our souls because we believe it is the secure thing to do, or staying in a relationship that is abusive because it is all you know. If you venture outside of the boundaries there could be danger out there. The reality is, it is more dangerous to stay in the place where your soul is unable to grow than it is for you or me to take that step of faith.

To begin to even imagine taking steps outside of your comfort zone, you must realize how your mind works. Each time you and I have a thought or act out a behavior we create neural connections in our brain. Have you ever driven somewhere countless times, maybe to work or school realize you were on autopilot half the time? That has happened to me on numerous occasions. I remember a specific incident where I was driving to a place that I frequented often. I had so much on my mind and my thoughts were preoccupied. I pulled into the parking lot and realized that I had been unaware the entire time of my driving. It was as if I was completely on autopilot. My brain had gone into default mode. The neural connections were so deeply ingrained in the tissues of my brain that I didn't even have to think about that behavior.

The same thing happens with the way that we think. If you or I believe a situation to be fearful, uncertain or potentially dangerous, we will, by default, avoid it. This could be in many different ways. Have you heard of people being afraid of success? Why on earth would anyone be afraid of success? Because, somewhere along the way this person developed a thought pattern that connected success with pain on an unconscious level. Unaware that this thought pattern has taken root, a person will actually sabotage their own success and are not even aware of why they are doing it.

In order to change this pattern you and I must become crystal clear on what it is we want and why we want it. This creates awareness. Once you are aware, you can begin to create strategies that will stop the behavior that can potentially destroy your destiny. You begin by changing the way you think. You don't even have to physically do anything. You only need to change your thought patterns. For example, when you are experiencing something that brings you pain, stop and think about why you are experiencing this pain. I am specifically referring to emotional pain. Are you fearful? If so, why? Is the fear justified? Do you doubt your abilities? If so, why? Should you? If you are honest, do you need to prepare more or receive additional training? Begin to move the thoughts from the subconscious area of your brain to the frontal cortex, where you have to reason and think. By doing this, you can begin to change the neural pathways in your brain, leading to different thought patterns. Earl Nightingale in his famous book, *The Strangest Secret,* (1956) speaks of a

30 day challenge. The 30 day challenge involves thinking constructively on your own behalf. Have the courage to think positively about your very own situation. Think only in positive results. If you are seven days into this process and you begin to be engulfed with negative thoughts and worry, start over again. It is by doing this consistently that we begin to take steps that move us from fear to freedom. We are able to take more courageous steps of faith outside of what we perceive to be our safe zone where we are, by default, comfortable, but not growing into our greatest God gifted potential. I challenge you today to begin to think positively on your own behalf. Begin to vision what your life will look like if you attempted that which you were afraid of failing.

A word to all of you who are holding tight to your vision, despite the currents that threaten to take you under, I applaud you. You my friends, are life's true champions. Continue on in your quest to die empty. To use all that you have been gifted to enrich the lives of others.

Take Action

1. **Be real with yourself about what you are avoiding.**
   Too often we avoid situations, people, events that we perceive as painful. In order to avoid the pain as I spoke of in the first chapter, we simply avoid what it is we need to face. The pain is inevitable. You and I cannot live a full life without discomfort. The more we run from it the more pleasure and life satisfaction will elude us. Giving us a false sense of reality that if the source of pain, perceived pain even, is avoided, it will simply disappear. Unfortunately, that is not the way it goes. Take out a piece of paper and write down what it is you are avoiding getting real with, that is causing you pain or emotional unrest in your life. It might not be something that is in the forefront. It could even be something that you can push to the back of your mind. It is time to bring it out into the open. There is no reason why you should struggle with discontent. Yes, there are times in our lives that we are struggling and figuring out what to do next. This should not, and I repeat, this should not be the norm for you or me. I have found while working with

clients, and even in my own life that when these issues are not addressed we are pretending they do not exist. The reality is they do exist and like a festering pimple, they will pop up and come to head. Once again, by doing this, by avoiding looking at these issues square in the face you are staying within your comfort zone. Like Dorethea Brande said, you are willing yourself to fail.

_____

_____

_____

_____

_____

_____

2. **Identify one action step you can take this week.**
   I am a firm believer in taking massive action. I am also a realist. You can actually sabotage your own efforts if you try to move outside of your comfort zone too quickly. What will happen is that you will take huge strides, feel the tinge of fear, and slowly creep back. To avoid that from happening, it may be best for you to identify one action step you can take this week. Yes, I said week. You read that correctly. I did not say daily. That will come later. Start small. Start strong. In his book, *The Compound Effect* (2012) Darrin Hardy says that small action steps that are consistent are the foundations for true and lasting change in our lives. I couldn't agree more. Pick one thing. It could be making a phone call you have been avoiding, believing that it is going to be a painful experience. Each time you take action on what you know to be the right thing, you win. You take a step to freedom. Get comfortable with being uncomfortable one step at a time. Once you have taken that step into the unknown realizing you aren't going to die, you can feel it out for a while. Celebrate your victory. It truly is a victory. As Thoreau said, too many people live their lives in quiet desperation. They are not physically dead, but are dangerously close to an emotional death. That is no way to live. You and I are created for so much more. But to get to that "so much more" you need to move outside of what you perceive as comfortable and begin to

take risks that will strengthen you. So, what is that one thing you need to do right now?

_____

_____

_____

_____

_____

_____

CHAPTER 3

The Fear and Doubt Factor and Other Grand
Illusions of Defying the Impossible

> "You gain strength, courage and confidence by every
> experience in which you really stop to look fear in the
> face. You are able to say to yourself, 'I have lived through
> this horror. I can take the next thing that comes along.'
> You must do the thing you think you cannot do."
> — ELEANOR ROOSEVELT

You are created and prewired to succeed. You and I are born with only two fears, according to science. These fears are put in place to protect us from outside danger. The two fears are, the fear of falling and the fear of loud noises. Every other fear we have has been learned. Most, if not all, of your fears have been learned. You and I did not come into the world with them. Most likely these fears were developed and ingrained into our minds over a long period of time; possibly taking years to develop. The good news is however, that you can unlearn them. You do not have to live a life of fear and self-doubt. You can live a life of victory if you are strategic and intentional.

There is a particular condition in psychology that has always fascinated me. This condition is termed, *Learned Helplessness*. The theory of learned helplessness was conceptualized and developed by American psychologist Martin E.P. Seligman at the University of Pennsylvania in the late 1960s and '70s. While conducting experimental research on classical conditioning, Seligman inadvertently discovered that dogs that had received unavoidable electric shocks failed to take action in subsequent situation. Essentially, the animal felt helpless. The stimulus, or painful experience was repeated over and over with no escape for the poor creature. At first, the dog tries to get away from the pain, but, to no avail. Once the he realizes that all of its attempts are futile the dog simply gives up. Eventually, adopting the will to stop trying to avoid the stimulus and behave as if it is utterly helpless to change the situation. Even when opportunities of escape are presented, this learned helplessness will prevent any action. Although this concept has been strongly tied to animals, it can be directly related to humans as well.

Learned Helplessness for people can best be defined when we feel that we have no control over a particular situation. This situation could be anything, really. It could be a physical environment that is dangerous. It could be a situation, relationship or environment that is dangerous not necessarily physically, but mentally and emotionally, stealing our very essence slowly day after day. At first it is uncomfortable. We may even make an attempt to leave or remove whatever it is that is causing discomfort. If an individual is displaying *Learned Helplessness,* they may behave in a helpless manner. By helpless manner, I mean that this person believes they have no control over a person, thing or circumstance, so why even try controlling it. Quite possibly, they have tried to escape or remove themselves from whatever it is that is causing pain; yet, when their attempts are consistently thwarted, they give up. At first glance my mind takes me to an individual who is in an abusive situation and helpless to leave. And, this could very well be. However, this condition can happen to a person who is in a job that is less than fulfilling. Maybe this job does not pay very well, or what they are doing is in direct opposition to what they value most. It could be that this person is not using her potential to the fullest yet feels trapped due to life's responsibilities. Slowly, day after day, a quiet desperation sets in and life becomes heavy and joyless.

This inaction can lead people to overlook opportunities for relief or change.

Consider one often-used example: A child who performs poorly on math tests and assignments will quickly begin to feel that *nothing* he does will have any effect on his math performance. When later faced with any type of math-related task, he may experience a sense of helplessness and refuse to even try.

Learned Helplessness has also been associated with several different psychological disorders. Depression, anxiety, phobias, shyness and loneliness can all be exacerbated by learned helplessness. For example, a woman who feels shy in social situations may eventually begin to feel that there is nothing she can do to overcome her symptoms. This sense that her symptoms are out of her direct control may lead her to stop trying to engage herself in social situations, thus making her shyness even more pronounced.

Learned helplessness is so subtle that we may not even be aware that it exists in our lives and even more dooming, is keeping us from living to our greatest God-gifted potential. We accept certain ways of thinking, behaving, or being treated in a certain way as normal. Why? Because that is what we are used to; it is within the realm of our comfort zone. It may be good. It may even be bad; yet, it is all we know. Knowing is comfort. Not knowing represents uncertainty and this uncertainty places us in a state of consistent discomfort. I find that too many stay in prisons out of fear. The prison I am referring to is not a physical prison. The prison I am referring to is the prison we create in our own minds and hearts. God never intended for anyone to be in a prison. His gift is freedom; freedom to live the life that you were created to live.

When you are feeling helpless remember this comforting scripture and know in your very soul that God is on your side.

> *What, then, shall we say in response to these things? If God is for us, who can be against us?* (Romans 8:31, NIV)

If God is for you, there is nothing on earth that can prevent your success! And, God will never leave your or forsake you.

> *"Those who know your name trust in you, for you, Lord, have never forsaken those who seek you."* (Psalms 9:10, NIV)

You and I can have confidence to move into uncertainty with boldness and joy.

My Epic Fail

Do you believe that fear can be used to motivate? Had you asked me that several years ago I would have said that fear could never be used as a motivator. How could such a terrible monster as fear be used to motivate a person and cause them to step into their God gifted potential? Before I explain just how that is very possible, and even necessary, let me explain a little about fear.

Fear sometimes gets a bad rap. Rap sheet a mile long. However, some fear is healthy. Yes, healthy. As a Motivational Speaker, I get nervous before I speak. It doesn't matter the audience or venue. I still get nervous, even fearful. Not all fear is created equal. We need some amount of fear to keep us on our toes, to inspire us to move and function on and with all four cylinders. The right amount of angst can keep us fresh and on our game. You can get butterflies in your stomach, just make sure they are all flying in the same direction.

I am firm believer in preparation as well. So often we see others as having it all together and it comes so easy and natural to them. Most likely this person has spent years honing their craft. What we see is only the tip of the iceberg. Below is a strong foundation that took years of training, going through obstacles and a lot of tedious mental work to enable them to do what they do so well. Let me share a story with you that will bring light to how fear can truly be a motivator and a catalyst for progress.

While listening to a main speaker at a dinner event celebrating community and business support for the career development of the local youth I suddenly became very ill. Not because the speaker was so bad, but because of a memory that surfaced in my conscious mind after years of lying dormant.

Five years prior to that event, in late August, I was the Keynote Speaker for an Educational Conference in the very same room and stood at the very same podium. I have considered the entire experience an epic failure. Certainly one of my worst. The kind of professional failure that one can hold onto for months or even years. Potentially leaving you crippled with fear, indecision and even doubting your own professional abilities. As I was being called to the podium I remember my stomach suddenly writhing in a fit of knots. I walked nervously forward, took the microphone, looked out at the audience of 500 and froze. I stood immobilized by fear, not one word was coming out of my mouth. I looked at the event coordinator, glanced at the clock (I was supposed to speak for 45 minutes) and felt a hint of vomit begin to emerge. For one split second I considered walking away. Fortunately, I chose to stay, reluctantly. I spoke for 43 minutes and do not remember one word I said. I also remember vividly vowing I would never experience that again. It completely and utterly terrified me.

I can say with absolute confidence I have not. I have not experienced that moment of terror and mental frozenness since that day. It is not because I have never spoke in front of an audience again. Quite the opposite. I used that very experience to motivate me to step up my game and become better at my craft. The very craft I believed deep in my soul God was calling me to.

I was not about to tell Him, "I think I will pass on the Life assignment, Lord. Can I pick another one?" I have since gone on to speak multiple times all over the United States. I have received standing ovations and have seen people in my audience cry because my words moved their very soul. Had I decided to let fear win, how many lives would go untouched? How would the course of my life and the lives of others be altered? The same is true of you. You have a gift. You were born with potential that is bursting at the seam, waiting to be fully realized. Yes, it is scary. Yes, you will feel fear. Yes, you may even fail. I do know one thing for sure, you will survive. You will bounce back. You will develop the ability to be stronger and more confident each time you do not back down from a challenge. Eleanor Roosevelt said it best when she said, "Do something every day that scares you." That's how you and I become less afraid.

Obstacle or Opportunity?

One of the greatest threats to our future is the unknown. What is out there? What awaits me if I take this chance or make this change? Would it be best if I just stayed right where I am? After all, I know what to expect here. Someone or something may hurt me if I venture too far away from my comfort zone.

I consider myself a bold and confident woman. However, there are times that I get too comfy in a place that I know in my soul, God wants me to move out of. I sense it. I feel the knowing of His Will for me, yet I am afraid. What is on the other side of this unknown? Is it good? Is it dangerous? Will it destroy me? Will I have to work harder? I have found it is during such times of mental pinball that God pushes me out just as a mother bird pushes her babies to make them fly. Stepping outside of our comfort zones is challenging on a normal day. Most of us, if we admit it, would not take the step willingly. If you are like me, you like being in the safety zone. It feels safe. And as human beings, we are all about safe and secure.

There are times when we are forced outside of our zones. At first, we leave kicking and screaming. We don't like the outside view. It is unfamiliar and the territory has not yet been pioneered. No trail to follow and certainly no light to guide us. As a motivational speaker and life coach for women who are experiencing transition or a stuck point in their lives, my moto is and will always be, "Every obstacle can be turned into an Opportunity". The problem however is that every so called "opportunity" is not always a welcomed opportunity from the surface. It has been my experience that the very best opportunities can come clothed in shock and pain. Opportunity can come when we least expect it, leaving us dazed and confused. When we are in these, moments it is more than challenging to right ourselves and balance the blend of emotions that are seemingly on the verge of exploding in a fit of toxicity.

We ask ourselves questions like, "Where on earth is the opportunity in this." We may even stomp our feet and shake our fists, pouting like a child.

The Apostle Paul experienced many obstacles, yet as scripture unfolds we see that these very obstacles were only opportunities in disguise. The Bible tells us that Paul was a very talented and intelligent man. Paul held a prestigious position and one where he personally persecuted the Jews, God's chosen nation. He was a man who was certainly on the wrong course in life. That is until God personally saw to it that his life take a new direction. And a new direction he did take. Paul is the author of many books in the Bible and in the last half of his life preached the Gospel of Jesus Christ with passion and conviction. Paul was an intellectual, in the Roman military and not afraid to take bold steps into whatever venture he was headed. My mental picture of Paul is a man of great stature and composure; both feared and respected by those who knew him. He definitely knew what his purpose was and was willing to carry it out no matter the cost. But the Bible talks about a "thorn" in Paul's flesh. It is not specific about what that thorn was. It could have been anything really. Yet this thorn caused Paul a great amount of pain; emotional and mental anguish is my guess. He implored God to take it away. He asked three times. Now stop and think about that for a moment. Here is a man of great accomplishments. What he says he will do, he does. He does not back down from a challenge. Most likely he grabbed the challenge by both horns and wrestled it to the ground. That is the picture the scriptures give of the Apostle Paul. Yet here he is, pleading with God to take away this thorn. Observe the text from 2 Corinthians 12:9 after Paul had implored God to take this thorn away.

"But he said to me, "My grace is sufficient for you, for my power is made perfect in weakness." Therefore I will boast all the more gladly about my weaknesses, so that Christ's power may rest on me." (NIV)

Considering that I am not a studied theologian, my view on Paul's thorn was that he truly believed it interfered with the call on his life. But God, this omnipotent God, saw otherwise. Observe the dialogue where God tell him, "No." He tells Paul, and He is telling us, His Grace is sufficient for whatever we are going through. There is nothing too great that we cannot handle while we stand in the middle of God's will for our lives. It is through these very trials that our character is shaped and molded into the very image of Christ. So much of stepping outside of our comfort zones is a bold and courageous act of faith. Faith in the One who created you and believing that His Grace will uphold you and keep you safe. Grace is defined as the unmerited and undeserving favor of God. When you and I have favor with God we can move mountains my friend. So, that is why we rejoice when we experience opposition of all sorts. It is the gym of life. Training us to be warriors in our own lives and the lives of others.

I didn't see that coming! Or did I?

It was the middle of summer and we were just wrapping up another successful Fourth of July Holiday. The Fourth of July has always been my favorite holiday. I love it because it is summer, which means it's warm, there are tons of gorgeous fireworks and we are often surrounded by dear friends and family. This particular summer was no different. Well, there was one exception. This was the summer I was all-in commitment and focus on launching my speaking and coaching business. I had decided that the time was here and now to begin the journey that I had put off far too long. The time to grab hold of what God had promised me was now. Not tomorrow, not "someday", but now. This is what I wanted and I could no longer stay on the fence and wonder if it would ever happen for me.

George Bernard Shaw says, "People are always blaming their circumstances for what they are. I don't believe in circumstances. The people who get on in this world are the people who get up and look for the circumstances they want, and if they can't find them, make them!"

For the past year I had been in a relationship with individuals who were thriving in their business and loving every minute of it. I have to admit I was somewhat envious. I wanted that for myself. Yet, if I looked deeply and honestly into my day to day activities, it was apparent that I was not doing what they were doing to get where I needed and wanted to be. I was Mom, Wife, and had numerous other things that called for my attention. At least, those are the reasons I would console myself with to avoid the nagging reality that I was making excuses. I was far from lazy. Yet, my activities were not pointed in a focused direction and my goals at that point were still unclear. In order to step confidently outside of your comfort zone, your goals need to be crystal clear. Ambiguity only hides our doubt and fear. Clarity is the fiery dart aimed at purpose.

For the past decade I was a workshop facilitator and speaker for a large state agency in addition to teaching four college courses. I was busy, but not focused. I was busy, but not fully committed to my entrepreneurial goals. My income was covering our mortgage and all of the extras our family needed. It was just inside my comfort zone. Close enough that I could see the outside, but far enough that I was unable to make the leap.

July 1st is always the beginning of a new fiscal year for the particular agency that I was contracted with. I had recently signed a contract for the next two years, but there are never guarantees in the world of government money. I knew, and have always known, that my contract could be pulled at any time. I was extremely good at what I did. Each workshop evaluation brought stellar reviews. I got along famously with the staff in each county office and I was just about the most ethical person on the planet with it came to any job that I was assigned.

As June progressed, I had heard no word in terms of my summer schedule. Summer schedules were booked three months in advance. I'll admit, I was concerned. This job, after all, was paying my mortgage. It was comfortable. Not challenging or rewarding, but comfortable. Two meetings were planned with the *Powers-that-be* (Executive Director of said Agency) to discuss scheduling and possible new opportunities, only to be cancelled at the last minute with suspect reasons. As July 1st came and went, my concern went from level one, not too bad, to level 10, code red. In a desperate, but not wanting to appear desperate, attempt to retrieve answers, I shot out a quick email to the particular power that was to determine my fate. The correspondence was straightforward. In other words, "What is going on? Do I have the contract or not?" is what I said. My heart was beating somewhat when I hit the send button on the email. Almost as if not sending it would just make all of this discomfort go away. How we fool ourselves.

The response came within the next thirty minutes. I saw it in my inbox, taunting me like a playground bully; "Open me! Open me!' it seemed to scream. I gave in and opened it immediately. I felt like I was handing over my lunch money. Below contains all the juicy details:

Dear Julie,
Blah, Blah, Blah and lots more Blah's!
(I needed to cut to the chase.)
I checked with "so and so" (code for the highest power that be within the agency) and "so and so" said we are not going to have you do workshops for us during the summer. Well, ever again actually. You will never, ever return in like one million trillion years. Your job here is gone and your life is over. You may have to move out of your house now and wear a burlap bag as a dress. Oh, and you will have to use coupons at the grocery store.
Yours truly,
So and So
Otherwise known as, "The Executioner"

I may have embellished somewhat, but that is what my mind made it out to be. "So and so" did not actually say those things, but the message was similar.

That was it. In one email I lost the money to make a house payment. My safety net was yanked out from underneath me, followed by the words, "Have a nice summer!" Really? I, of course, being a confident female entrepreneur, who teaches other women to be confident women, did the most professional and confident thing I could think of; I cried, called my Mom and looked for a great big jelly filled doughnut. Not necessarily in that order.

Suffice it to say that I did move on from that experience. I can say with truthfulness that it was an obstacle turned opportunity. It was not a smooth transition by any stretch. Yet, a transition nonetheless. Life is full of transitions. I remember hearing a speaker say, *"Life is all about letting go."* After I heard that I pondered that thought and realized just how right he was. So much of our pain is self-inflicted by trying to hold on to something that we need to release and let go. By letting go we allow other robust life changing opportunities to enter our lives. It is almost as if we mentally let go and in the letting go we are able to have better vision to see opportunities before us. Our perception is, in fact, our very own reality. If we are able to make peace with the *letting go* of life, we will live much calmer and happier lives.

Shortly after my contract ended, I received a call from an agency in a city nearby who was in need of a trainer for a weekend leadership seminar they were having. I spoke to a very kind woman whose voice was that of an angel. Thank you kind angel for paying my mortgage for the next few months. It was completely out of the blue and not something that I had strived for. It happened, I am sure, by divine appointment. I choose to see the obstacle as an opportunity to grow and step into areas much bigger than where I was playing. I believe it was in this mental shift that produced the opportunity. You may be skeptical when you read this. I understand that. I believe in miracles and I believe in a God who promised to provide all of my needs. I hustle every day towards my goal. God has provided the vision and provision and fully expects me to honor that vision with a defined set of goals and action steps. By having a defined goal and a plan not only for your day, but for your week, your month, your year and even five years from now, you are able to dismantle fear and doubt. Action is one of the most effective keys to anxiety and depression. So go ahead and take action today. I believe in you. I believe that you can do the impossible. You have been given gifts and talents that only you can utilize effectively. Do not let fear or her evil twin, self-doubt, stop your destiny.

#Redemption

It was early October of 2014 and football season was in full swing. It is the time of year in Michigan where the leaves begin to change into brilliant colors, there is a chill in the air and winter clothes that have been packed away are being brought out in anticipation for the long winter season. This particular fall had a dark and gloomy feel. In the small town where I reside with my family, the high school football program was struggling. During the summer training months, there were rumors of cancelling the Varsity Football Program and concentrating on Junior Varsity by strengthening their numbers that had been getting lower each year. As with every high school sports team there are good years, triumphant years and some not so good years and seasons. The later was turning out to be one of them for our Varsity Football team. Sadly.

As the season progressed the boys had played a handful of games and with each one injuries were mounting. Along with physical injuries were the signs of mental fatigue fueled by bad attitudes, fear and doubt. The vision for the rest of the season was dimming with each devastating loss.

It was a cool Thursday afternoon and my son, Noah, who was a junior came home early from practice. He reported to me and his Dad that the coaches told the players they may need to cancel the rest of the season. The numbers were dwindling daily and momentum had halted to a slow crawl. I could see the look of disappointment in his young eyes. Not only disappointment, but a look of hopelessness as to what to do or even say. The decision, he said, would be finalized the following morning. It was not a waiting game.

The following morning came and I waiting anxiously to hear the news. It came via text message at 8 am from my son.

"We cancelled the season, Mom." Read the text.

I was beyond disappointed. I love high school football and my son is a gifted athlete who was preparing for a college football scholarship. The decision to cancel the season was not in his favor for recruiters.

The following week the entire community was in an uproar. Plastered all over social media were rumors of why the season was cancelled and a lot of blame and extremely disheartening comments about our boys, the coaching staff and the school district. I was so angry I had to consciously decide to not look at any social media to protect my mental state of mind. The New York Times called the school district's Superintendent to run a story as did the L.A. Times. Our high school football team was plastered all over the national news. The boys were devastated, felt defeated and were beginning to lose confidence and hope, not only in themselves but in the entire system that was structured to support them as young men and athletes. The negative energy permeated the entire community slowly robbing our athletes of the will to be champions. It was painful to watch and painful to experience as a Mother of a young warrior.

In January of the following year, a young man approached me about rallying our disheartened troops and getting these young men involved in a training program to prepare them for the following season. Intrigued, I agreed to meet with him. Joe, owns a Cross fit gym in our local community and has a heart to serve. Rather than complain about the problem, Joe wanted to find ways to be part of a solution. In early January, Joe and I gathered a team of concerned citizens, who also chose to be part of the solution and began to brainstorm how we could help our Football team make a comeback. One of the reasons for the cancelling of the 2014 season, and the decrease in numbers was due to the high amount of injuries. That was the first issue of business at our very first meeting. What can we do to decrease the amount of injuries and strengthen our young men to be able to compete? The seeds of vision began in that first meeting. Joe and I along with the Varsity Football Head Coach, Todd, a man dedicated to his team and truly a man of integrity, were the only three at our first meeting. The vision that began conception was that next season, and seasons to follow the team and boys would grow stronger, both mentally and physically. Each one of us could see it. We could envision it in our minds eye, the window of the very soul that victory could and would be had.

In January, 2015, the entire Varsity Football team began training at Joe's gym three times a week. This continued for the next eight months with a consistent attendance of 32 young men. Even during the summer months, when training began at 6:30 am, the attendance never dipped below 28 warriors. The boys created a Vision Statement for their team; "New Year, New Team, One Dream" as well as a word to describe their focus,

#REDEMPTION

Redemption being defined as the act of redeeming or of reclaiming something. The boys and the community were on a mission to reclaim what was rightfully theirs. As for our small group, we eventually turned into a non-profit that functions to this day with the sole purpose of providing strength and agility training for the Varsity and Junior Varsity Football team. What began as an incredible obstacle, turned into an opportunity to take a stand against complacency, fear, doubt and adversity, boldly looking it in the eye and saying,

"Not today! Courage wins on this day and every day moving forward."

The months passed, the boys worked diligently and with a mental tenacity that was mind blowing. The first Varsity Football game was scheduled in late August. Our first competitor was a team the boys played the beginning of last season and the results were devastating. It was a blowout. The boys were facing them once again. However, this time was different. This time the young warriors were prepared and had been in intense training for eight months and two weeks. They were ready for battle.

The night of the first game was amazing. The entire community came out to support the team and surrounded them with confidence and inspiration. Each one of us were for them. We believed that they could do this. We believed that visions and dreams could become a reality with dedication, hard work and mental fortitude. I wish I could say the game was easy, that our boys went out onto that field and crushed the other team. That did not happen.

The boys went out onto that field that warm August night with confidence in their minds, hearts and souls. Confident that they had the community behind them, their teammates with them and the knowledge that they had been working for this day for a very long time. The game was not easy. Every yard, every catch, every tackle and down came with blood sweat and tears. But, they came. Slowly, one after the other. Never giving up. Never giving in. Never losing sight of the goal. The final score of the game,

26-24. Our boys triumphed by two points. A team that had stomped them into the ground the year before was now under their feet, by two points. The victory was sweet and deeply heartfelt. The boys cried out with pure joy and excitement as the community rushed onto the field to embrace them. It was a coming home of sorts. Coming home to victory that is attained by first seeking a vision, believing in that vision and shutting out any fear that threatens to dismantle the vision.

What is it that you have given up on? What is keeping you from your victory? What have you "cancelled" in your life because you are injured and too tired to continue? I urge you not to give up. You have what it takes to be victorious over your circumstances. You may not believe it now. You may not be able to see it. Not yet anyway. Yet, it is there. It has been with you all along. It just needs to be worked out by intense training, dedication, support and a never, ever give up mindset.

Oculum in metam is Latin for *the eye on the goal.*

What is your goal, your vision, your very life's mission?

"Let your eyes look straight ahead; fix your gaze directly before you" (Proverbs 4:25, NIV)

Take Action:

1. **Define what you fear:**
   I mean really define it. What exactly are you afraid of? So often what we fear will never happen. It is the story we tell ourselves. As humans we tend to live in the past or in the future. The past is gone. The only thing that the past can do is haunt us with memories of what we perceived happened. The future is not yet here. The realities of our future are suspect at best. The Bible tells that our lives are like a vapor. Here one minute and gone the next. Live in the present moment. Take your "right now" by the horns and tame that pesky rascal. When we live in the here and now, yesterday and tomorrow are not as scary. I like to write things down. Not type them, but actually physically write them. When you have

movement you are able to gather information for various parts of your brain. The right side of our brain is big picture thinking and visual. The left side of our brain is linear in nature. Check the boxes type of thing. Write or draw your fear and be very specific. For example: "If I don't write this proposal correctly I will not be awarded the contract". I realize that is extreme, but you get my drift. Write it out. Once you do, you may realize it has very little power over you.

_____

_____

_____

_____

_____

_____

2. **What is the worst possible thing that could happen?**
   After you have written all of your fears about a particular situation, write next to each one the worst case scenario if your fear was to become a full grown monster. Which of course, it most likely will not. Once again, be very specific. Say it out loud if you have to. Using the above example, here is how that may look; "If I do not get this contract I will die by midnight." Get raw and real with yourself. It's only you reading these, so do not be embarrassed. Dig deep into your soul and be authentic with yourself. For some, this may be the first time you have been 100% honest with how you truly feel.

_____

_____

_____

_____

_____

_____

3. **If the worst case scenario happens, what exactly am I going to do about it?**
   Let's assume for arguments sake that the very worst possible scenario does in fact happen to you. What are you going to do? Are you going

to run away and hide? Give up on life? Bury your head in the sand and never come out again? I highly doubt that. Here is what you can do to take control of not only this situation but overall, your destiny. Devise a plan of how you will now proceed. Give yourself specific action steps along with a definite timeline of when these will be accomplished. If you can avoid it, do not take more than 10-14 days to decide a plan of action. If you take longer, you may slip into the trap of indecision which is a very dangerous place to be. It is there you lose all momentum. Even though I failed college physics, I do remember this, an object in motion tends to stay in motion and an object at rest tends to stay at rest. Stay in motion. By doing so, you are not giving in to the feeling of fear. There is a difference between feeling the fear and dealing with fear. If we live our lives dictated by our emotions, we will be tossed to and fro by any dark circumstance that comes our way. If we learn strategies to deal with the fear, we can pull from our foundation and stand tall during a storm. James tells us to ask for wisdom liberally because it is given freely.

> *"If any of you needs wisdom to know what you should do, you should ask God, and he will give it to you. God is generous to everyone and doesn't find fault with them. When you ask for something, don't have any doubts. A person who has doubts is like a wave that is blown by the wind and tossed by the sea. A person who has doubts shouldn't expect to receive anything from the Lord."* (James 1:5-7, NIV)

_____

_____

_____

_____

_____

_____

4. **Define your personal #Redemption.**
   What is it that you want to redeem and bring back to life? Define what it is and write it down. Take some time to sit in a quiet place

to be alone and begin to ponder what it is that you have cancelled in your life. It is your birthright to redeem what the enemy has stolen from you. As a child of God, created in His very image, there is nothing that you should be cancelling out that is part of your victory and destiny. Inside of you is the raw seed of potential waiting to be nurtured so that it can give birth to the greatness that it holds. Too often we become discouraged and fearful that maybe it won't happen. There has been too much injury and the healing process is long, painful and agonizing. By injury I am referring to emotional and mental injuries that may have been no fault of your own yet you are feeling the after effects of the assault. Or it could have been a poor choice that you made and the consequence of your actions have lasting effects. Please know that no one is perfect.

"All have sinned and fall short of the glory of God" (Romans 3:23, NIV).

It is through Christ and His sacrifice on the cross that we are forever redeemed. That is the truest meaning of redemption. It is not God's Will that you and I live a life under injury, too immobile to live out His purposes for your life. He is inviting you into the gym with Himself as your personal trainer to strengthen you each and every day so that His blessings may be sustainable in your future.

Grasping hold of your very own personal redemption will cost you a price. Nothing worth having and holding onto is free. It will not come easy, nor should it. If it came too easily for you, you would not value it. Define today what your redemption is and create a plan to redeem that which was lost.

_____

_____

_____

_____

_____

CHAPTER 4

"Yeah, But........." A Standoff with the Chatter Box

> "The brave man is not he who does not feel
> afraid, but he who conquers that fear."
> — NELSON MANDELA

It was a beautiful June summer night. I could feel the breeze coming in through the window as the curtains waved back and forth. I was already in my P.J.'s and ready to settle in for the evening. Madison, my oldest daughter was spending the night at a friend's house, Noah was with his Grandmother, and my youngest, Zoe, a toddler and already in bed sound asleep. It was the time of the evening I could relax and let my mind wander away from the events of the day, which were usually stressful. Chris and I have three beautiful children, born within a four year period. Having children young and so close together is a wonderful and joyful experience, but at the same time can produce a great amount of stress.

For as long as I can remember I wanted to be a stay-at-home Mama. Rather than drop my babies off at a day care center every day while I headed to the proverbial office I wanted to be the face they saw in the morning and after a restful afternoon nap. Chris and I both made sacrifices so that could become a reality. It was not always easy, yet it was the right choice for us and our family.

However, somewhere during those years I lost myself. I lost the essence of the woman I thought I was or the woman I had always dreamed of becoming. It was almost as if I sat in paralyzed silence as she slipped away day after day. The dreams that I had in my teens and my early 20's were a fading memory. I remember being sad almost every day. Could it have been hormones? Yes, I suppose it could have been. Yet it was a prevailing fog that never ceased to surround me. Happiness was something that eluded me. My relationship with my husband was almost non-existent. He had his life and I had mine. His involved his job, friends and projects he found to do in the garage. I felt increasingly isolated in my own home.

I remember that June night like it was yesterday. I sat on the couch that faced the open window. I could hear the sounds of summer, the neighborhood children playing and in the distant background the hum of the TV that my husband was watching in the other room. It was a typical evening for us both. Separated physically in different rooms, but more so, separated emotionally. I felt an intense sadness wash over me. The kind of sadness that makes your gut ache. I hated that feeling. It was all too familiar to me. I wanted to avoid it at any cost. I shook my head as if to say to myself, "Snap out of it woman!" With that I hopped off the couch with a bounce in my step suddenly remembering the bottle of wine I had bought earlier that day. Heading towards the kitchen, I grabbed the wine opener in the silverware drawer on my way to the cupboard to retrieve the wine and one glass. Using both hands to carry my booty my eye spotted an Avon catalog. Suddenly I decided there was no better thing to do on a warm summer night than to drink wine and order make up. At the moment that was absolute nirvana for me. I bent down and picked up the Avon catalog with my teeth and headed back to the couch. Once I had my glass of wine poured, I settled in to view the entire Avon catalog.

The last thing I remember was reaching for the bottle of wine to pour another glass, only to realize it was empty. I had drank it all as I was gleefully picking out all of my goodies in the Avon catalog. I grabbed my phone and quickly dialed Sue, my wonderful Avon representative. I do not remember much of the conversation, but I was quite confident that I did place my order. I then closed my eyes and fell sound asleep.

The next morning came all too quickly. By that time all of my children were home, the house was bustling with activity and I had a hangover. I blamed it on the red wine, but the truth was I had drank too much the night before. The deeper truth was that I was beginning to drink every night. I knew in my inner most knowing that I had a problem, but was not willing or able at that point to face it. Sometimes, we are not able to face the reality of our situation. Sometimes, God in His mercy will keep us in His arms until we are ready and able to begin the healing process. Hopefully, before permanent damage has been done. In my case, it was very close.

The next week as I was leaving the grocery store my phone rang and with one hand I tried to reach it in the deepest bowels of my purse. My attempts were unsuccessful and I missed the call. Finally I located the cellular device to see who had called. It was Sue, my wonderful Avon representative. I quickly called her back eager to pick up my order.

"Hey Sue. It's Julie. I am assuming you called about my order?" I inquired cheerfully.

"I sure did! I can drop it off or you can pick it up. Where are you now?" She asked.

"I am leaving the grocery store so I will swing by and grab it if you are going to be around. How much do I owe you? I have some cash on me, but I might need to write a check is that okay?" The truth was, I had no idea how much I had ordered. My memory was still foggy from that night.

"Yeah, I will be home. Stop on over. Your total is $157.89." She squealed with delight. I believe her delight was in part because she made more in commission on my single order than she had in the entire last month of sales.

I don't think I spoke for what seemed like an eternity when in reality it was 10 seconds.

"Julie? Are you still there?" She asked, sounding concerned.

I could hardly speak. I was in shock. How on earth could I have spent $157.89 on Avon? Was I out of my mind? What did I buy? Could I send it back? Was it all the same thing, like 15 shades of blush? What?

"Ahhhhh, yea I am still here. I have to go to the bank so it is going to be a few extra minutes. That ok?" I said in a very somber tone.

"Oh sure! I will wait for you." She squealed again. I bet she would wait. She made a killing off of me.

As I drove to the bank to take out $157.89 from our family's checking account, money that would buy food for my children, I was so sick I almost had to pull over.

How could I do that? How could I have let it go this far? What happened to me? Tears began to stream down my face and I sobbed uncontrollably. I felt completely and utterly alone at that moment. As I pulled into the bank parking lot, I sat for a long, long time, crying. Letting out sobs of anguish and desperation. Years of pent up anger and sadness came rushing out of me. It was a terrifying experience; and at the same time, it was also very healing. It is difficult to explain. I had reached the bottom. I had lived for too many years in blind misery, covering up my sadness and anger with alcohol and drugs. I knew in the very moment I could not go on like this any longer. I needed help and I needed it now.

It has been years since that day in the car. I can still remember the feeling like it was yesterday. I don't even remember who that person was. She is a distant memory for me. After that day I immediately got treatment for my addiction. I wish I could say it was an easy and seamless transition but it was not. Far from it. It took months for my heart, soul and mind to heal. I have never worked so hard at anything. I was literally fighting for my life. Fighting for the one life that I had been gifted and realized that I was so close to throwing it all away. It took time, energy, tears and so much emotion to heal the relationships that had been severely damaged during that time. The relationship that suffered the most was the one I had with myself. I hated myself for what I had done. It was a long journey to forgiveness and learning to live in the present and make way for a bright and prosperous future. God was, and continues to be incredibly good to me and I held on to the scripture in the book of Joshua,

> *"Have I not commanded you? Be strong and courageous. Do not be terrified; do not be discouraged, for the LORD your God will be with you wherever you go."*(1:9 NIV)

Are you running?

What in your life have you been running from? What in your life, if you are completely honest with yourself have you been covering up because it is too painful to face? Your cover up may not be as drastic as mine, but nonetheless, a cover up. Covering up an issue or issues we face is no way to live; certainly not the way God intended for us to live. We are created to live full and abundant lives. When we feel emotional pain or a low grade fever of discontent it is a sign that you need to pay attention to. We are not promised a life of ease, but we are promised a life of peace if we are centered in the Will of God for our lives. Pain left unattended will turn to depression. When we become depressed, because we want more than anything to get away from the pain we, we will do whatever we can to move away from the negative feelings. Too often they are short term solutions that only leave us more empty and disillusioned in the end.

In my case, I could have lost my life, my family, everything that I held dear. When I look back over that time I almost shudder. It would be easy for me to wallow in guilt and regret, which if not kept in constant check, would serve only to keep me looking backwards rather than looking forward to the amazing future that God has promised me. If you, like me, suffer from guilt or regret about things that have happened in your past, I urge you to ask God to release you from that. Focus your thoughts on what you can do and who you are becoming now. Your past in no way will determine your future. The best we can do is learn from our past mistakes and create a compelling future for ourselves and those we are privileged to serve. Believe it or not, your past obstacles can in fact turn into your greatest opportunities.

From Misery to a Mission

I can look back at those years in my life with shame and guilt or I could look back and see grace and mercy. I am forever thankful that I was able to get through those years and not suffer severe consequences. I can say with absolute certainty that all things do in fact work out for our good. God is able to take such a devastating circumstance and turn it into something only He can use for His glory and victory. Because of that experience I am more empathetic and nonjudgmental to other people and what they may be going through in their lives. So often we stand in judgement based on what we think should happen or how we think things should be. How selfish that is. All of us are simply trying to get through life and do the very best we can. That experience, those years of utter emotional chaos prepared me for the journey I am on today. God turned my misery into my mission. I now have the unique and wonderful opportunity to view the world and circumstances through a lens of compassion. You can rise above whatever it is you feel chained to. Whatever your prison, there is a way out. God is with us during our trials and our temptations.

"No temptation has seized you except what is common to man. And God is faithful; he will not let you be tempted beyond what you can bear. But when you are tempted, he will also provide a way out so that you can stand up under it." (1 Corinthians 10:13, NIV)

There is hope my dear friend. You can turn your obstacle into an opportunity to launch into some of the greatest years of your life. It all starts with the chatter box in our own minds.

One of the biggest obstacles to success is our own self-talk, which I refer to in this context as the chatter box in our own minds. Our minds are filled with our own chatter. Is the chatter productive or does it speak negativity over your life? Are you prophesying death to your circumstances and you are unaware that there is slow decay happening day after day? Proverbs tells us that our power truly lies in the words we speak,

"The tongue has the power of life and death, and those who love it will eat its fruit" (18:21 NIV)

I was prophesying death to my own life. I was speaking very unkind things to myself and about my life. I was blaming everyone and everything else for my own self-induced misery. If my husband had paid more attention to me then I would not have had a problem with drugs and alcohol. If my kids were better, I would then act better. If we had more money I would be satisfied. If I had more support from friends and family I would not have made such poor choices. The list goes on.

Maybe if some of my circumstances had been different, I would be different. Yes, that is a possibility. How long will we wait for our circumstances to change before we make the leap and decide we are just not going to take it anymore. Turn off the negative chatter box in your mind and get some new verbiage. Begin to speak life over your circumstances and watch how they begin to come alive. As you turn off the negative chatter and tune into the positive and life giving chatter, you are viewing the world through a much different lens. You begin to see opportunity where all you could see was an obstacle blocking your way. You become more grateful for the gifts you have been given. When you become more thankful you begin to cherish your life more. Realizing it truly is a gift. Treat yourself and others around you more kindly. Your life and the lives that surround you possess incredible value. Treat them as such. Do whatever it takes to begin to turn off the negative chatter and replace it with life giving phrases. By speaking life into your circumstances you are giving fuel for a bright and prosperous future.

Stinkin Thinkin

The problem of my addiction did not begin when I started numbing my pain with substances, the problem was conceived when my thoughts began to give birth to the negative thoughts and feelings. I nurtured each one by giving them room to grow and develop a deep root system in my mind. That is why it took me so long to get well. It had been so long that I had let those thoughts dominate my mind that it took a lot of work on my part to rewire my brain and think right. God never intended for me to think that way about myself. Remember, His thoughts are thoughts of peace and prosperity for me and for you. We need to get in alignment with what God is thinking about us. Whatever He thinks is always the right thoughts.

> Jeremiah 29:11, *"For I know the plans I have for you,"* declares the LORD, *"plans to prosper you and not to harm you, plans to give you hope and a future."* (NIV)

Begin to trust what you know to be truth, rather than what you feel in a temporary moment of distress.

Our feelings are poor indicators of the reality that God planned for us. It is a trick of the enemy to fool you into thinking you have no hope and no future. That is a lie from the very pit of hell. The battle we wage is within our minds, not in our outward circumstances. Paul speaks very plainly about this in his letter to the church in Ephesians.

"For our struggle is not against flesh and blood, but against the rulers, against the authorities, against the powers of this dark world and against the spiritual forces of evil in the heavenly realms" (Ephesians, 6:12, NIV).

We fight a battle that we cannot possibly win in our own strength. Our strength must come from the One who is our Creator. He, and only He, knows the weight that we are capable of sustaining during times of trial and pressure. He will never let us bare weight for which we are not equipped. However, we have a responsibility to do our part. Our part is to become so acquainted with the Truth that comes directly from the Truth Giver that when a negative thought comes into our minds, we quickly let it go. Never entertain such thoughts. The temptation is great, yes, but the consequences are devastating. Consider the words of Paul once again,

"Finally, brothers and sisters, whatever is true, whatever is noble, whatever is right, whatever is pure, whatever is lovely, whatever is admirable--if anything is excellent or praiseworthy--think about such things" (Philippians 4:8, NIV).

God knows full well that in order for us to stay connected to Him, to His Truth, to His thoughts of us, we need very desperately to stay connected to the thoughts we think. The chatter in our minds will either lead us to life, or it will lead us to death.

You changed my life

Recently my husband and I went out for dinner. Our usual place was closed so we decided to eat at the local restaurant and bowling alley. Not our normal choice but we decided to try it. When we walked in every table was full so we decided to eat at the bar. We grabbed the only two seats left and waited for the waitress.

"Hi!" she said. "What can I get you to drink?"

"I will have a water and he will have a coke." I smiled as I spoke. No wine for me. I had that lesson down pat.

She smiled back and kept eye contact for longer than usual. I felt a little uncomfortable, like maybe I had spinach on my teeth or something worse. Off she went to get our drinks. When she returned she placed two napkins on the bar and put our drinks on top of each. She turned around and stopped as if she was thinking. She then turned back and stared right at me with a slight grin on her face.

"You don't remember me do you?" She asked.

I was completely thrown off guard at that point. I took a sip of my water and replied, "No. I am sorry but I don't. Should I?"

"I attended one of your workshops about three years ago. The ones you were doing at the college." She responded.

I thought for a moment. I hadn't done workshops at the college for quite some time. "Boy that was a long time ago," I said, "Can you give me more details."

"I don't remember the name of the workshop, but I remember you." She said as her gaze lingered. "I remember you because you changed my life that day."

I just sat there and stared at her.

"Yeah, I remember the words you said that day and the way you said them. You gave me hope. You gave me hope that my life was going to be ok. That I was going to be ok. I will never forget that." And with that she walked away to grab another order.

I sat stunned. I could feel the tears in my eyes and my husband's blank stare in my peripheral vision. "Wow!" He said.

"Yeah, wow." I responded.

I will never forget that night as long as I live. Ever. Every obstacle that I have ever gone through and survived to tell about it with a victory stance, was worth it. My mess had turned into someone's miracle. My trauma had enabled someone to find triumph and I wasn't even aware that it was happening.

Never forget that your life matters. What you do and what you say has an impact on more lives that you know. It all begins with what you tell yourself. What you believe about who you are, why you are here and what you can accomplish. Begin today to turn off the nega-tive chatter and speak life to yourself. When you speak life over your own mind and soul, you are enabled to speak life into someone else's circumstances.

Take Action:

1. **Begin to become aware of what you are telling yourself on a daily basis.**

   Les Brown, a very popular and dynamic motivational speaker, said that over 80% of what we tell ourselves is negative. Isn't that amazing! Women speak on average 25,000 words a day, out loud. Imagine the words that go through our minds each day. My guess is that that number is tripled. So, 80% of what you and I tell our-selves, sometimes at an unconscious level, is negative. Do you want to change that? Can you imagine what your life and outside circumstances would look like if you changed that 80% to posi-tive self-talk? Yours and my life would look drastically different. In order to make that become a reality, we need to be fully aware of what we are telling ourselves. Science tells us that we will act on what we believe and we believe what we tell ourselves. If I tell myself I can't, then I believe that I can't. My actions will be a direct reflection of my belief system. If I begin to change the negative self-talk in my own mind to that of a "can do" attitude, my actions will be a direct reflection of my belief system. There is no reason for you to stay stuck in a vicious and negative cycle of thinking. I refer to it as "stinkin-thinkin". The best way to get out of that cycle is to become cognitively aware of what you are thinking on a daily basis. This can be a challenge at first, but well worth the effort, I promise you. You may have to write down on paper the thoughts that you want to be thinking about yourself and about your future. Read them out loud three times a day. Keep them in places where you can see the phrases. It takes on average 21 days to change a habit. Just to be safe, I always give it 30 days. Make it a point to take a

30 day challenge to change your thinking. You will be amazed at the results.

_____
_____
_____
_____
_____
_____

2. **Develop an attitude of gratitude.**
The best way to begin to think positive thoughts is to be very aware of all that you have been blessed with. To not only be aware, but to think of these things the moment you wake up in the morning and your feet hit the floor. If you have to, make a list and look at that list whenever you begin to feel a negative thought. Rather than think of all the things you do not have, focus on the things, the people, the opportunities you do have. It is the subtle lie of the enemy to trick us into believing we do not have enough, that other people have more than we have and then we constantly compare ourselves to other people. You are right where you need to be in this very moment. God has a plan for your life. He is a gracious and abundant God who wants to bless and prosper us. In order for you to be able to see all that He has for you, you need to begin by seeing all that He has already given you. It is then you will see the opportunities that await you. Make it a daily practice to be grateful for the blessings you have in your life at this moment in time.

_____
_____
_____
_____
_____
_____

3. **Never compare yourself to others.**
One of the most devastating things you can do is compare yourself to others. Have you ever done that? I have, too many times. I feel

the envy begin to creep into my mind. It starts small at first with a slight feeling in the pit of my stomach. The kind that feels wrong and uncomfortable. In my mind I sincerely want to be happy for this person, who could very well be my friend, and their success. I want to rejoice with them because I know that in my rejoicing will come my own success as well. Yet, sometimes it is difficult to do. I give into the temptation to wallow in self-pity. Self-pity begins to conceive the seed of self-doubt. If I am not careful this self-doubt will turn into discouragement, and quite possibly, fear. Fear is an emotion that will cripple any creative energy you have. The best way that I have found for myself and the clients that I have coached, to avoid the comparison trap is to focus on yourself. I certainly do not mean that in a selfish way. I mean to focus on the gifts, talents and abilities that God gifted to you when He thought of you.

"Before I formed you in the womb I knew you, before you were born I set you apart; I appointed you as a prophet to the nations." (Jeremiah 1:5 NIV).

That is amazing! God knew you, He knew me before we were even formed in the womb. You are special and possess many unique gifts and talents that God fully intended for you to use for His glory. By walking in your own gifting and talents, which are often referred to as passions, you will not feel the need to compare yourself to others. Each one of us is gifted to do amazing things and to make a difference in the world. You will make that difference in your own way. If you are unsure of your unique talents and gifts, ask God to help you. Ask Him to reveal to you what you are good at and how He wants you to use those during this time you have on earth. James tells us to ask God for what we need because God will give it to us.

_____

_____

_____

_____

_____

_____

CHAPTER 5

The Belief Factor: Creating a New Normal

"One of the greatest discoveries a man makes,
one of his great surprises, is to find he can
do what he was afraid he couldn't do."
—HENRY FORD

Webster defines normal as: according with, constituting, or not deviating from a norm, rule, or principle or conforming to a type, standard, or regular pattern.

I want you to think about your life and how, up until this point, you have defined normal for who you are and where you are now. Have you been so caught up in a particular norm, rule or principle that you have never questioned its authenticity? Do you find yourself surrounded by others who think like you? Dress like you? Are as smart as you? Make about the same amount of money as you? What if I told you that you don't have to stay in the normal that you have grown accustomed to. Would you believe me? Or does the thought of that scare you? Unfortunately, we are creatures of habit both physically and psychologically. We stick close to the borders of our comfort zone, not wanting to veer too far from the shore. We sense something is out there that could, in fact, be very good for us; yet, we are unsure how to attain it. Lost in a fog of confusion as how to move forward into a life of destiny that was promised to us by our Creator.

In Matthew Chapter 16 Jesus teaches his disciples a valuable lesson regarding living in a new normal.

Jesus had just had a conversation with the religious leaders of that time, the Pharisees and Sadducees in regards to seeing signs and miracles. The religious leaders were seeking to test Jesus. They were not interested in seeing signs and miracles, they were simply interested in their own agenda. Shortly following that conversation, Jesus and His disciples got into a boat to go to the other side of the lake. While in the boat the disciples realized they had forgotten bread for the journey.

"When they went across the lake, the disciples forgot to take bread. "Be careful," Jesus said to them. "Be on your guard against the yeast of the Pharisees and Sadducees." (Matthew 16: 5, 6, NIV)

The chapter goes on to say that the disciples reasoned or discussed among themselves as to why Jesus would come out of the blue and say that. They thought he was chastising them because they had forgotten bread for the trip.

"Aware of their discussion, Jesus asked, "You of little faith, why are you talking among yourselves about having no bread? Do you still not understand? Don't you remember the five loaves for the five thousand, and how many basketfuls you gathered? (Matthew 16: 8, 9, NIV)

Jesus went on to remind the disciples of how often He performed miracles for large amounts of people with small amounts of food. He uses two specific examples; one where He fed 5,000 men with five loaves of bread and a few fish and the other when He fed 4,000 with only seven loaves of bread and a handful of fish. As if that was not enough, there was food left over for the disciples to collect in baskets. Jesus was not talking about bread in the physical sense at all, but was referring to being very careful as to not let the Pharisees and Sadducees influence their thinking about what normal is in the Kingdom of God. He was gently reminding them of all that He had done and how normal that was for Him and how normal He wanted that to be for them as well.

We get so used to the way things have been and currently are in our lives and our outside circumstances that we have a difficult time perceiving that life could and in most cases, should be different than it is. You and I are meant to soar and not get stuck in outside circumstances that only serve to deter you from your destiny and the very purpose that God has for you. It is not His intention that you live below your potential. But before you and I can do that, we need to examine our thoughts to see if they are in alignment with what God has spoken over our lives. Do you remember the parable of the talents? When the master came back and discovered that the servant who had only one and hid it, he was angry. The Master took that only talent he had and gave it to the one who had ten. How unfair you might think. Not at all! You see, that is a new definition of what we have been culturally been taught to believe. In God's Kingdom, if you have more, you need to increase it. There is plenty to go around. Do not hoard your talents in fear that they may one day be taken from you. When you and I do that, the ironic thing is, we only lose them. The reality is, we are all born with *more*. You have more talent in you right now than you can imagine.

I remember very vividly after I began to come out from underneath the fog of addiction and negative thinking that had so consumed my life, that what I was seeing was not what I wanted to see. I had surrounded myself with other individuals who were likeminded and also stuck in an addiction. The addiction may not have been chemical in nature, but it was an addiction nonetheless. Addicted to staying in a bad relationship because it was comfortable. Addicted to thinking negatively about a particular situation or person. Addicted to staying in a job or career that was not challenging or using their gifts and talents to the absolute fullest. By staying stuck in an addictive cycle we begin to develop a dependency on our excuses. We tell ourselves that we are this way because of this or because of that. If we hadn't grown up in that particular home we wouldn't be this person. If we would have had support for our dreams and ambitions we would be further than we are now. Those sound very good on the outside. They are all socially and culturally accepted reasons as to why we did or why we are not living to our fullest potential. When in reality they are excuses and rationale as to why we are not where we want to be. Some people hide behind them for years. Some even go to the grave with their excuses.

What do you believe?

One of my favorite stories and one that has brought me a great amount of inspiration is the story of the legendary Roger Bannister and the four minute mile barrier. Born to working class parents in March of 1929, Roger's opportunities for the future were limited at best. When an individual grew up in a poor part of the country career prospects were most likely confined to similar paths as parents and grandparents. Yet Roger Bannister had always aspired to more. He was the type of person who had a vision of possibilities before they were a reality in the natural. At a young age, Bannister often set seemingly impossible goals for himself. As a gifted runner, he earned accolades from his peers who in one breath would tease him for being too studious and in the next praise him for his ability to run and run fast. Bannister was particularly gifted in running the mile. His goal was to run the mile in under four minutes; a feat that had never been done. Until this time, medical experts believed that if a man ran a mile in under four minutes their heart and body would explode. It was believed the human body was simply incapable of pulling off any type of physical achievement to that extent. Yet, Bannister refused to believe this. He believed that it could be done, and he was going to do it. Roger Bannister refused to believe it was impossible.

On May 6, 1954 in a meet in Oxford, England, competing for the British Amateur Athletic Association, Bannister broke the four minute mile barrier running the mile in 3:59.4. The unbreakable record had been broken. At the finish line, Roger collapsed with exhaustion. Medical doctors and bystanders rushed to his aid thinking that he had collapsed and his heart exploded. That was not the case. Bannister was fine, just tired. Within eight weeks, 16 other runners had broken the four minute mile barrier. Today, hundreds of others have accomplished this feat. They are even doing it at a high school level. What changed? Did Roger possess some type of super human strength? Why hadn't it been done before that day in Oxford? The truth is, nothing changed; nothing in the physical realm that is. The change took place deep in the part of the mind that believes in possibilities. Belief that the impossible can and will be possible. A new *normal* had been created that day in early May.

During an interview Mr. Bannister had this to say about human achievement and potential in overcoming what is perceived as impossible.

"It wasn't, in my view, physical, but it did become to some extent psychological. And it was really an example -- I don't know whether the

*word paradigm is correct -- paradigm of human achievement in a
purely athletic sense. What limits are there to what the body can do?"*

What is it that you believe to be possible or impossible for your life? What
your current surroundings tell you what is and was isn't possible. Could
it be that this mindset is simply a manufactured state to keep you in your
comfort zone? Could it be that there really is so much more for you avail-
able that you have not yet tapped into due to your limited belief system?

The Bible is very specific about how important our belief system is in
relation to what we can achieve. Jesus spoke of this multiple times during
his three year ministry. Look at this verse from Mark, Chapter nine verses
21- 23. The back drop of these verses tells us of a man who is bringing his
demon possessed son to Jesus. It appears by the text that the father is doing
this as a last resort, exhausted from dealing with the situation and really not
believing that the boy's situation could change.

*"Jesus asked the boy's father, How long has he been like this? From child-
hood, he answered. It has often thrown him into fire or water to kill him.
But if you can do anything, take pity on us and help us. If you can? Said
Jesus. Everything is possible for one who believes."* (Mark 9:21-23, NIV)

Do you see the father's question to Jesus, *"BUT,* if you can do
anything..............."

He doesn't sound very confident does he? It sounds almost as if he has
given up hope of anything every changing.

Sound familiar? Do you ever get that way? I know I have. When I begin
to feel this way it is so easy to gravitate back to my comfort zone. To seek
those things in my life that are easy and comforting to all that I perceive
as safe, secure and the false sense that what I have known is the best I can
ever hope to achieve. I am fearful and even skeptical that what may lie on
the other side of my discontent is any better than what I am in now. I have
often asked myself, "What if what I am seeking beyond this is worse than
what I have?" When this belief system is left unattended and allowed to
run rough shot over your thinking system it can and will lead to a vicious
cycle of doubt, fear and a double mind. If you are suffering from this you
may feel things like, a low grade fever of discontent, a pervasive sadness,

confusion or the inability to make decisions with confidence. Worst of all you will lose the ability to tap into your creative power and the playful kind of spirit that accompanies such thinking. The first chapter of James speaks of the dangers of not believing you can achieve what you not only ask God for but believe you can have.

"But when you ask, you must believe and not doubt, because the one who doubts is like a wave of the sea, blown and tossed by the wind. That person should not expect to receive anything from the Lord. Such a person is double-minded and unstable in all they do." (James 1:6-8 NIV)

Believe that what you desire in your heart is possible. Believe that what you can see right now is not all there is to life. Believe that you are capable of creating a new normal for your future; you can have more and be more.

Who or What is Your Goliath?

When you look at a dismal situation or are facing an ugly obstacle what do you see? What do you believe to be true about your ability to overcome and turn that seemingly insurmountable obstacle into one of the greatest opportunities for your success and ultimate destiny?

The story of David and his battle with the Philistine, Goliath is a great example of believing and trusting not in your own strength, but that of God's. Remember that God is the one who created you and He knows the weight that you are capable of sustaining under pressure. This story is a shining example of paying attention to the unique gifts and callings of God. David and Goliath's encounter occurred during the standoff between the armies of the Israelites and the Philistines. If you are familiar with the story, Goliath stood over nine feet tall and stood taunting the Israelites to send someone from their army to fight him. Needless to say the soldiers in the Israelite army were quite intimated. Saul was the King of Israel and Commander and Chief of the Israelite army. He called the shot. What happens, however, when the one who is in charge is afraid? Here is a conversation between Goliath, a major player in the Philistine army and the Israelites. The he is referring to is anyone who has the courage to fight him.

> *"If he is able to fight and kill me,"* Goliath shouted, *"we will become your subjects; but if I overcome him and kill him, you will become our subjects and serve us."* (1 Samuel 17:9, NIV).

The Bible tells us that upon hearing these terrifying words from such an intimidating giant, Saul and his army were terrified (verse 11, NIV) Specifically the Bible uses the word dismayed. The word dismayed literally means the breakdown of courage and thoroughly disheartened. Have you ever felt that way? Have you felt that your courage leaves you and you look up to the heavens and call out to God for strength? I can imagine that is the way King Saul and his army felt.

Goliath continued to taunt the Israelites for forty days leaving them paralyzed with fear to the point they could not even respond. This is when young David arrived on the scene. David was summoned by his father, Jesse, to take food to his brothers who were fighting with Saul. When David heard what Goliath was saying he questioned the soldiers. Most likely thinking and pondering in his own mind why these valiant soldiers were so afraid. David's response to Goliath's threats was this,

> *"Who is the uncircumcised Philistine that he should defy the armies of the living God?"* (1 Samuel 17:26, NIV)

David knew deep in his heart and mind some very important factors. The first is that David saw Goliath as a mere mortal who only possessed mortal abilities and had many limitations. Goliath was not invincible. Secondly, David recognized the value of his own unique experiences in defeating the enemy. He also recognized his own unique gifts and talents. David, a mere teenager, a Shepard boy, was more willing and ready to accept the challenge.

As David stepped out to meet the challenge, Saul objected,

> *"You are not able to go out against the Philistines and fight him; you are only a boy, and he has been a fighting man from his youth."* (1 Samuel 17: 33, NIV).

David's response was to remind Saul of his victories thus far. The victories that he believed with all of his heart came directly from God's strength, power and might. David tells Saul,

> *"Your servant has killed both the lion and the bear. This uncircumcised Philistine will be like one of them, because he has defied the armies of the living God. The Lord who delivered me from the paw of the lion and the paw of the bear will deliver me from the hand of the Philistine."* (1 Samuel 17:36-37, NIV)

David was only a shepherd, and Saul was King of Israel. You would think that the one who would be brave in the face of fear would be the King. David knew that it was God who provided him strength during this challenge. Saul had forgotten that. I love this conversation between Saul and David as David is about to go and fight Goliath.

> *"Saul said to David, "Go, and the Lord be with you."*
>
> *Then Saul dressed David in his own tunic. He put a coat of armor on him and a bronze helmet on his head. David fastened on his sword over the tunic and tried walking around, because he was not used to them.*
>
> *"I cannot go in these," he said to Saul, "because I am not used to them." So he took them off. Then he took his staff in his hand, chose five smooth stones form the stream, put them in the pouch of his shepherd's bag and, with his sling in his hand, approached the Philistine [Goliath]......*
>
> *As the Philistine moved closer to attack him, David ran quickly toward the battle line to meet him. Reaching into his bag and taking out a stone, he slung it and struck the Philistine on the forehead. The stone sank into his forehead, and he fell face down on the ground.*
>
> *So David triumphed over the Philistine with a sling and a stone; without a sword in his hand he struck down the Philistine and killed him.* (1 Samuel 17: 37-40, 48-50, NIV)

Who or what is your Goliath? Are you facing an obstacle today that seems impossible? What do you believe you are capable of? One thing is for sure, do not attempt to overcome a barrier or obstacle without the power and the strength of your Creator. Remember that He has called you to a divine destination. Whatever He has called you to, He will also equip you to do. We tend to forget that when we are in the midst of pain and difficult circumstances. That is when we have to remember it is not by might and not by your own power, but the God's Spirit that we are able to move forward despite the Goliath that stands in our way threatening and taunting to take us down.

You and I are the most strong when we embody the person God created for us to be. You do possess the strength to move forward, if only you will dig deep for the lessons that you have learned and the experiences you have had that God has so mercifully brought you through. It is during those times that our character is developed. ThePsalmist, reminds us to stay strong;

"..........*weeping may stay for the night, but rejoicing comes in the morning*" (30:5NIV).

Believe that what you truly want for your life is possible. Because it is.

The wealthiest place in the world

The late Myles Monroe once asked a very compelling question during one of his sermons. He asked his audience, "Where is the wealthiest place in the world?" As I listened, I was on the edge of my seat. My mind was spinning with possibilities. Of course, your answer is completely dependent on how you define wealth. Think about that long and hard before you attempt to answer. Wealth in this sense means increase with what you and I already possess.

Referring back to Matthew chapter 16 again, Jesus makes a statement to His disciples that has huge implications. He asks them in verse, 26,

"*What good will it be for someone to gain the whole world, yet forfeit their soul? Or what can anyone give in exchange for their soul?* (NIV).

What can you and I possibly give in exchange for the unique gifts and talents that God gifted us before time began?

You may be asking yourself, what does that have to do with wealth? It has everything to do with wealth. Remember I asked you how you define wealth. Let me refer back to Dr. Munroe's answer to the question, "Where is the wealthiest place on earth?" His response to that question was, the graveyard. In the graveyard are bodies that once contained a person and their very essence, their soul. Within that essence were gifts and talents that had been given to them before time began. God placed inside each one of us very a very special assignment. Your life is the most precious commodity in the world. You and I are only gifted one life while we are here on earth. There are no dress rehearsals before the final show. Inside of you may be a book, a business, a community, lectures, and paintings, whatever your talents are. Are you using them to their fullest capacity? Or, do you complain that your life has no meaning or your life is too hard? When you and I can shift our perspective and realize that hidden in each one of us is amazing wealth, we then begin to see the new normal that God had planned for us all along. A life of struggle and discontent was never the master plan of God. We are created in in His very image. As we begin to shift our thinking and realize we have been buying into the lies that the enemy has been telling us, a new world of possibilities will begin to open. You will begin to sense a freedom to move into a new dimension of success and creativity. You have more than what you can see. You are so much more than what you can see. It is time that you start to live that way.

Five Rock Stars

The late Jim Rohn talks about the importance of surrounding ourselves with people who will encourage, uplift and be real with us when we need it. I cannot express enough the value of having the right peer group. Mr. Rohn teaches that we are the average of the five people we spend the most time with. You and I will either rise to the level of our immediate peer group, or we will sink to their level. As human beings we have an intense desire to be in relationship. Not only be in relationship, but have those relationships be harmonious. Even at an unconscious level we will begin to behave like our peer group. You will begin to take on the mannerisms, the culture, and certain customs including economic status. If you are hanging out with millionaires you will begin to think like a millionaire. Consequently, if you are surrounding yourself with individuals who are continuously making excuses as to why he or she cannot seem to hold down a job, repeatedly getting "let go" from jobs or who never seems to make enough to get ahead, you will begin to think and act the same way.

This type of mindset can cover all areas of life including relationships, education, future outlook, and self confidence level. As you begin to create a courageous life and start stepping outside of your comfort zone, as you ease away from what was normal to you, and into another realm that defines a new normal, you will be amazed at what you begin to see. So much of what you begin to recognize was in fact there all along. You were simply looking at your outside circumstances through a different lens. You may find that the peer group that you once were satisfied being with during your down time, no longer seem appealing to you. You may have started to think differently and are wanting different things for your future. You may even find that you are spending more time alone, simply reflecting on your life and where you want to go next.

Being alone is very valuable. It can be a time of deep reflection and soul searching. When you are able to be alone with your thoughts and not be fearful of that, you have certainly come along way. Getting to the place where you need time alone is very healthy. It is in these times that we learn to not simply react to the outside circumstances, but we begin to plan and strategize based on what we truly want and desire. It is only when you can take regular time to do this that your life will begin to be shaped and crafted as it was designed. In addition to time alone, is spending time in the presence of God and listening to His voice and His direction for your life and future. Remember it is God and God alone who knows the future. What better way to plan than with the one and only who knows what lies ahead for you?

Letting Go

As I began to change my thinking and develop daily habits that were much healthier both physically and mentally, I had to take a very hard look at the people that I was choosing to surround myself with. I once heard Bishop T.D. Jakes say in a sermon that he could tell who a person was most influenced by simply by doing an inventory of their cell phone. In other words, who you and I are going to emulate are going to be the people we share our time with. I took those words to heart and began to evaluate what influences I wanted to have the greatest impact on my future. It was during this time that I had to make some difficult choices and let go of a number of relationships that were very, very dear to me and had lasted for many years. It was not that these people were bad people or had done anything that was malicious or to hurt me. The deciding factors were the language they consistently used about their life and circumstances, the excuses they held on to for being stuck in the place they were in and the negative way they spoke of others and even of themselves. Once I changed my thinking I realized how destructive such habits were and the devastation it can have on your future. Of course I made every effort to persuade my friends that there was a much better way to live. I was sure they could see the changes in my life. Or perhaps they could not. Just maybe they could not because when I was with them I was acting just like they were and that, for me, was dangerous.

It was then I realized I needed to cut all ties. I wish I could say that it was easy. It was not. In fact it was emotionally painful. Yet I knew deep in my heart it had to be done. I asked myself if I was willing to tolerate acute pain in exchange for chronic pain. The answer was a definite, yes. I could rip that proverbial band aid off and get it over with, or I could leave it on and let the pain fester and continue to put off the inevitable.

I spent many lonely days feeling sorry for myself and wondering if I made the right decision. I knew in my head that I had, but my emotions were telling a different story. I had to be acutely aware that emotions will lie, and are fickle, only projecting what they know to be truth based on the current circumstances and not taking into account the larger vision. I did however, start to feel comfortable with myself, my thoughts and I learned to encourage myself when I had no one else to lean on. Most importantly, I learned to trust God and hear His voice above all others. To strategize a plan for your future this step is an absolute must. It is one you cannot skip.

Captain Underpants

It had been a particularly long day and I had spent the entire morning and the early afternoon in my office working diligently on a variety of projects that had certain deadlines. It was mid-July and very, very hot. Our home did not have air conditioning at the time and my office was an off shoot of a former bedroom and the room had no windows, which meant zero ventilation. I was becoming increasingly restless and knew that I needed to take a break or my brain would go crazy from overload. I quickly finished what I had been working on, saved it to my flash drive, shut the computer and headed to grab my running clothes. I had a million things on my mind so I vaguely remember changing from one outfit to the other. I think I was talking to myself the whole time as well. Something that is not out of the ordinary for me. Once dressed, I headed to the garage, grabbed my running shoes, laced them tight and headed out on my usual four mile route. The sun was shining and I immediately felt an endorphin release as my feet hit the pavement. Freedom at last. The familiar route takes me through neighborhoods and eventually downtown and home. I had just left my home and was passing by a neighbor's house when felt something was amiss. I could not quite identify it. I shrugged it off and kept running. I ran past a road crew and noticed the stares of the workers. I smiled to myself and thought, "Oh yeah, I still got it!"

Downtown was bustling with mid-summer activity and it felt good to be out of that stuffy office and breathing in fresh air. As I rounded the corner to the street I lived on I noticed that my new neighbor was outside taking care of her flower garden. She was a young woman, not quite five feet tall with long dark hair and big dark eyes. I had not had an opportunity to meet her and some of her mail had been delivered to my home. What a great time to not only meet her and introduce myself, but I can also deliver her mail.

Rather than go home I stopped at her house first, which was located directly across the street from mine. I introduced myself, breathless, from my run, and she smiled and said hello. I noticed that she was looking at me strangely. I felt it odd, since we had just met. Not only odd, but somewhat on the rude side as well. I told her I had her mail and would grab it and come right back. Once again, she smiled and nodded her head giving me the same strange look.

"What on earth is she looking at?" I thought. I was starting to become irritated. I ran home, grabbed her mail and quickly delivered it to her. She thanked me, gave me that smile, glanced down towards my legs and turned and walked away. I shrugged my shoulders, turned quickly and headed across the street to my driveway. Once I was in the driveway I slowed down to a walk. As I got closer to the front door I passed the big picture window that looks into our dining room. Because the sun was shining so brightly I could see my reflection as I passed by. What I saw caused me to stop dead in my tracks. In my haste to get dressed I did not realize that I had put my running shorts on inside out! I looked like I was wearing a running speedo. No wonder I felt as if something was amiss when I started out my run. It was. No wonder my neighbor looked at me with that strange look and the road workers probably thought I had escaped from the mental hospital.

Horrified, I called my husband to tell him what happened. After my breathless explanation there was silence. "Hello? Are you still there?" I asked.

"Yes. I am still here." He said.

"Oh my word! Can you believe I did that? I am so embarrassed!" I exclaimed.

"Jules, that doesn't surprise me at all." He answered back. "You better go back and tell the neighbor you didn't know, or she is going to think your nuts!"

We both laughed. I began to see how incredibly comical the whole thing was. I started referring to myself as Captain Underpants. I proclaimed that from now on I would start wearing my running shorts inside out on purpose and start a new trend. The entire experience is something I remember with fondness and it always brings a smile to my face.

Had that happened to me ten years ago I would have been horrified. I would not have come out of my house for weeks, embarrassed at my carelessness. Today, I can laugh at myself. I realize that it really isn't about me. The things that we stress about and think are going to last forever will one day be only a faint memory in the grand scheme of our entire life span. As a speaker I use this story in my talks that I give to both small and large groups about how we can get so caught up in the details that we miss the bigger picture. So much of our fear and self-doubt have deep roots in our self-centered view of the circumstances that surround us. Once we step back and see the bigger picture and how we fit into it, we get a better perspective and are able to make better decisions. The next time you feel a stressful thought taking hold of your mind, stop and remember that this may be a minor blip in the grand view. Bring that thought under control and remind yourself who you are, why you are here and that you have big things to accomplish.

Take Action:

1. Create a daily Mission.

What do you believe to be possible for your future? Are you stuck in survival mode or are you taking steps to thrive in your life. Be very careful of the lure to get caught up in the business of everyday life and simply reacting to circumstances that surround you. Too many people get distracted by daily "to-do" and the larger vision is lost. In order to avoid this trap begin to journal what you believe deep in your soul is possible for you. Do you desire a certain goal? Do you have visions of where you would like to be one day? When you see these visions in your mind's eye do you dismiss them as impractical for fear they will never materialize? Stay away from such thinking. Rather than have a "to-do" list for your day, create a theme or a mission for the day.

In big huge letters above my work computer I have the question, "What is your Mission today?" I look at it each time I sit down to work, whether it is answering emails, writing blog posts, creating social media content or writing a new book. Rather than what I have to "do", I reframe that thought to what is it I want to create? Amazingly this simple shift in language changes my thought pattern and gives me a new lens to look through. I approach my days much differently. As if each day is a new beginning to live my purpose and to make a difference; even if that difference is posting a Facebook status to encourage and inspire. For the next seven days ask yourself what your mission for the day is.

_____

_____

_____

_____

_____

_____

2. Define your Goliath.

What is your Goliath? I asked you that earlier in the chapter. We all have one. You cannot get through life avoiding an encounter with the proverbial Goliath. If you do, that tells me you are avoiding life all together. Define your Goliath by actually writing down what is the insurmountable event, person, or thing that is keeping your from living a full and abundant life that Jesus died for you to have. Did you know that God allows the Goliath to cross your path? He does this to prove that you are in fact capable of being an overcomer. You have the strength through Christ to slay any Goliath that comes your way. You do however need a strategy and you need to take action. David did. He had both strategy and action which he took swiftly and with confidence. Why? Because he knew that the living God was in his corner. The same God that was with David is also with you. Call upon His strength to defeat your Goliath. He won't do it for you, but He will provide the strength through you. Define your Goliath and ask God to provide a strategy for you to overcome and the courage to take decisive action. You will be amazed at the amount of confidence you will gain once you have taken steps towards victory.

---

3. **Who are you spending time with?**
   As Bishop T.D. Jakes said, you can tell who a person spends their time with, or may I add, who a person is most influenced by, by simply looking at their cell phone. Is it time for you to do a cell phone inventory? Who are the top five people that you are spending most of your time with? What is their character like? How do they like to spend their free time? What is the language they use regarding their lives, both in the present and future? Do they have goals and big dreams that inspire them to move forward with bold confidence? These are questions you need to be asking about your main influencers. You and I both have a choice about who we spend our time with. I urge you to choose wisely. Your very life and

future is on the line. This is no trivial matter. You will become the type of people you choose to spend time with. Make a list of your friends and take a serious look to see if these are the very individuals you want in your corner. I am in no way insinuating that you be cruel or have an attitude that you are in some way better than they are. Absolutely not. What I am saying is that your life has so much value and is so precious you need to take the utmost of care for it. That care involves what and who you allow to influence your mind, thoughts and visions of the future. Make a list today and decide if you need a new peer group. Pray and ask guidance from the very One who gives it freely.

_____

_____

_____

_____

_____

_____

CHAPTER 6

Like Nike says, "Just Do It"

"It is not the critic who counts; not the man who points out how the strong man stumbles, or where the doer of deeds could have done them better. The credit belongs to the man who is actually in the arena, whose face is marred by dust and sweat and blood; who strives valiantly; who errs, who comes up short again and again, because there is no effort without error and shortcoming; but who does actually strive to do the deeds; who knows great enthusiasms, the great devotions; who spends himself in a worthy cause; who at the best knows in the end the triumph of high achievement, and who at the worst, if he fails, at least fails while daring greatly, so that his place shall never be with those cold and timid souls who neither know victory nor defeat."
—THEODORE ROOSEVELT

It was the second time that Deb was going to be going before the "Sharks" to ask for funding to start her Women's Internet Radio Network. The first attempt was nothing short of a crazy mess.

In the summer of 2014 Bay City, Michigan hosted their version of, Shark Tank. You know the one on TV with the super cool and very wealthy business owners who are there to give the Poor *Start Up Dude or Dudess* a chance at living the dream. Picture that, but not in a big city in a fancy room with

TV crews all around. This was the Midwest, middle class American and a handful of potential rock stars all waiting for their 15 minutes of fame. There were six business owners, in the middle of a crowed and very loud cigar bar. Each one of the sharks is inhaling a burger and fries, drinking a beer and wearing really bad shoes. Can you say D-I-S-A-S-T-E-R? Deb was one of 15 hopefuls who were seeking money to begin a dream venture. Quite frankly, the whole thing was nuts. I attended, reluctantly, for the sole purpose of supporting Deb, my then business partner and radio show co-host.

I had met this woman a year prior at a Toastmasters meeting. We hit it off and decided to go into business together. The decision took approximately two days. True story. As a side note and word of advice, I do not recommend starting a business venture with a person you have had a few lunches with. However, that is the way I roll. I always have. I jump. Then I look. Has not always been a good strategy for me. I do have to admit there was an ever so subtle unease in my gut when I signed the paper. I ignored it. Quite frankly I was desperate to begin my dream. Desperate should never trump gut. And I mean, never.

So there I sat in the middle of the cigar bar. I could barely hear a word any of the want-to-be rock stars were saying during their 15 minute pitch. Then, after three grueling hours, Deb was on. She gave it her best shot asking for $3,000.00 in exchange for free advertising from these potential investors. She rocked and rolled that 15 minutes of fame and we all cheered. Sadly, the sharks did not bite. Afterwards I put my arm around Deb's shoulder, congratulated her and told her what a great job I thought she did. Very sincerely I might add. I consoled her with, "You will get them next time!" They were empty words of condolence never really thinking it would actually happen. That is just something we say to our friends and colleagues when things do not go as planned. Why we find the compulsion to do that is beyond me. It is like word vomit. It just came out and I smiled as I said it. You know the kind, the sincere fake smile that is really saying, "Holy cow you bombed that sister!"

Fast forward one month later. The Sharks were back and ready to rumble and possibly make a deal. I received a text message a few days prior filled with excitement. Deb was back in the game. When I hesitantly asked her, "Why the heck would you do that to yourself again?" Ok, maybe I didn't exactly say that, but I was thinking it, her response was this, "What have I got to lose?"

That is profound. If you remember nothing from this book, remember that and repeat daily if necessary. It is often when we get to these moments we begin to live a life with more boldness. Doing what we really want to do and saying what really needs to be said. Why? Because we have decided in our minds that the alternative of not doing what we really want deep in our hearts is worse. The alternative of not taking action is more painful than the act of taking a stand, saying the words, doing the deed. It comes out of our mouths as casual as if we are not connected to the outcome. But the reality is that the outcome has not become our slave. It is at this point that we have begun to master our perception of the outcome. That is true freedom. When the mental shift occurs to release our perception of how *it should be*, we begin to open up to possibilities of what *could be*. Our brains refocus. Searching for alternative ways to achieve our goals and fulfill our why and purpose in life. It is a beautiful thing. I was witnessing this transformation and was totally unaware. I was so locked up in my own perception of the outcome that I was unable to see the limitless possibilities that could potentially arise from this event. Monumental moment and it slipped right past me.

That night as she stood in front of the five sharks and an audience full of semi drunk and very loud patrons she confidently announced in the microphone, "I am asking for $5,000.00 to start my Women's Internet Radio Network." Following a long pause, she included, "I need a computer, microphones, a sound board and money to make a website. Up until now I have been doing it all myself. Oh, I need money to buy t-shirts and lots of them. I want to buy them in bulk because it's cheaper. In exchange, all of you can have 10% of our t-shirt sales." She had the biggest grin on her face I have ever seen. Keep in mind, the t-shirt sales at this point equaled $200.00 and that is at the high end. The Sharks were silent and just staring at her. Or, quiet possibly contemplating her incredible courage and sheer audacity. I could feel that feeling in my stomach. You know the one. It starts out small at first, turning into this raging monster and any moment you feel as if your face is going to burn off because you are totally uncomfortable with the awkward moment and silence.

Then it happened. The Shark on the end, the man with the gray hair and a very large draft beer and a cigar hanging from the left side of his mouth spoke. "I will give you $2,500 if my friend from the bank gives you $2,500.00. Then you will have your $5,000.00." I mean right out of the blue. Not a loan, but a gift. Deb stood there for what felt like an eternity. Once what he had proposed sunk in, she rushed over to the other Shark reached for his hand and shouted into the microphone, "Do we have a deal? Are you going to give me $2,500.00? Come on! Come one! Come on!" She ranted like an auctioneer that was making the sale of a lifetime. She ran up and down looking at each shark ranting, "Who is going to give me $2,500.00? Are you? Are you? How about you? "At this point the crowd was cheering as if we were at the Super Bowl with one minute left and the 49ers are one yard away from a touchdown in the 4th down. I could not believe what I was witnessing. The crowd began to cheer with their fists in the air shouting, "Give her the money. Give her the money!"

Suddenly a woman in the audience raised her hand in total victory and shouted, "I will give you $1,000.00!" The crowd went wild! Deb began to leap joyously as strange sounds came out from her mouth. Sounds I have never heard, nor hopefully, will I hear again.

When the dust settled and the crowd maintained some semblance of order, Deb was being ushered away by the "coordinator" of the sharks to gather her information and retrieve her booty. The announcer in the Hawaiian shirt was clearly stunned and oozed with an awkward type of giddiness not pleasant to witness. His crowd loved the banter and the mood was lively. In his excitement he chased Deb around the room asking if she would broadcast live from the very cigar bar we were in. He was like a child on Christmas morning. I had one of those moments where I literally had to shake my head and ask if what I was experiencing was reality.

I sat at the table with two friends who I could hear in the background giving high fives. I saw Deb out of the corner of my eye coming towards me with a smile the size of Texas. I hugged her and told her how proud I was of her and that she totally rocked and I had never seen anything like it. My words were with utmost sincerity.

On the way home that evening I went over the details in my head. Still in shock as to what I had witnessed. Something completely chaotic that literally worked out just as it should. The reality was, Deb completely put herself out there. Not once, but twice. She didn't over think what she had to do, she just did it. What she was saying did not make any sense to me at all. Why someone would give her money for that was beyond me.

Did you catch that? It was beyond what I thought should happen. I was only looking at it from my perspective. My perspective is not always accurate and I am only seeing it from one view. One view can be very one sided. Deb decided in her mind that her goal was important. That what she wanted was worth every penny she was asking for. She may not have had all the details worked out, but in the end it didn't matter.

Very rarely do we make decisions based on fact. We make our decisions based on emotions. How something makes us feel. Deb totally and completely felt that what she is doing and what she is about to do is the most worthy cause since toast and jelly, chips and dip, wine and cheese. It is a cause that will make the lives of countless women better because of her. Because she had that firmly in her mind, so did the sharks and so did the audience. It wasn't about them. It never was. It was about the cause, the goal, the almighty prize at the end of the rainbow. That is it. It's not complicated. Hold the goal. Know you are worth it. Believe you can do it. Take chances. Go for it. As Nike said, "Just do it".

Are you like Deb? Or are you more like I was in that moment? Do you hesitate when presented an opportunity? I am certainly not suggesting that you should jump on every opportunity. Every opportunity is not necessarily right for you and there are times that you need to be discerning. The problem begins when we become too discerning. You can say it is discernment when in reality it is fear. Fear that it might not work out. Fear that everyone will laugh at me and I will look like the kid in 8th grade who farted during the English Final Exam. Dead silence and suddenly a loud sound coming from little Jimmy's chair. You know the one, the distinct sound that cannot be passed off as a cough. That is the kind of embarrassment we feel deep in our hearts may happen. Who wants that? Not me. That is why I did not stand with Deb in front of the sharks. I kicked her out to the wolves because I believed in my head it would not work. Yet, I learned a great deal from that entire scenario.

Deb and I have since parted ways as business partners, but remain close friends even today. I will be an occasional guest on her Women's Radio Network, enjoying the comradery of likeminded women, interesting topics that relate in some way shape or form to modern day women's issues. Deb's original office was out of her home with a lap top computer, a head set and a hand written script. Now, she has moved twice and the last move was to a spacious office located in a downtown area filled with hustle and bustle of everyday life. I can tell by looking into her eyes when I see her she is filled to the brim with happiness and joy. She is living her dream. Never for one second doubting her ability to overcome and persevere in the face of insurmountable obstacles, much of which were her own self-doubt and fear. I have a certain level of respect for Deb and can say with all of my heart and soul I have learned many valuable lessons having shared time with this beautiful woman. This beautiful woman who began her dream after she retired. Evidence that it is never too late to begin your destiny.

I believe it is vitally important that we hold tight to the absolute belief that all of life is a learning time. A time for exploration and curiosity. The Bible promises us that all things work to the good for those of us who love God and are called according to His plan and purpose for our lives. (Romans 8:28) If you truly are living what you believe to be your life's purpose, mission and ultimate calling for your life, no devil or all of Hades can stop you. Why? Because you and I have the indwelling of the Holy Spirit. Hearing His voice and being diligent to obey His subtle prompts when we feel them in our being. I cannot impress upon you, the reader, enough that you and I are gifted one, only one, very precious life. It is up to each one of us to live that life in all of its fullness with abandon. Trusting that our steps are ordered by the very One who created us knowing full well what we are capable of doing, being and becoming. You and I are created in the very image of God. We have great big things to do in this world. Do not waste one minute in the quicksand of regret. If you are not careful you will slip so deep there will be no way of return. Jeremiah 29:11 states very plainly that God knows the thoughts and plan He has for our lives.

"For I know the thoughts and plans that I have for you, says the Lord, thoughts and plans for welfare and peace and not for evil, to give you hope in your final outcome" (NIV)

They are thoughts of good, not evil. Thoughts of prosperity and not poverty Thoughts are powerful weapons of warfare. We ultimately act on the thoughts we think about ourselves, our circumstances and the people we are in relationship with. Because we are created in the image of our Creator, what a powerful statement that is in the book of Jeremiah. God's thoughts of us are for a good and prosperous outcome. Prosperous in this context does not necessarily relate to monetary success. Being prosperous is so much more. There are so many people who have job that pay them a lot of money and afford them and their families to live in extreme comfort, yet are miserable in so many areas of their lives. True prosperity is the growth of your soul and your connection to the manufacturer of your being. Like a vine, we need that close intimate connection to the branch. It is then and only then that we know who we are and what our intended purpose is.

Should or Must?

One of the greatest joys of my profession, to which I refer to as my God gifted earthly assignment, is I get to be insanely creative. If you are familiar with personality styles, I am considered an extreme extrovert, highly creative and I like to jump into new projects feet first and consider the consequences at a later date. As a Life Coach and Speaker I know the importance of using your gifts to the fullest. Gifts can also be termed as strengths or talents. Trying to work on a weakness until it becomes a strength truly is a losing battle. Yes, we need to acknowledge our weaker areas, but if we focus too much on them we run head first into a battle of frustration. We are not designed to operate in our weaknesses. We are designed to be fully aware of our greatest strengths and capitalize on them each day.

I recently interviewed a man for whom I have a great amount of respect. His name is Joe. Joe is a bad boy turned good. He's young, early 30s, married with three kids. The reason I choose Joe is because he is a person who does what he believes to be the right thing. I am not referring to a moral or ethically right thing, although that is certainly the case with Joe, I am referring to the right thing being the right thing for Joe's soul. His ultimate calling and life's purpose. He is not one of the many who drowned out the still small voice deep in the place where your being is that whispers to you to move towards your joy.

In her book, *The Crossroads of Should and Must: Find and Follow Your Passion,* (2015) Ella Luna beautifully describes the difference between what we feel we should do and what we must do.

"There are two paths in life: Should and must. We arrive at this crossroads over and over again. And every day, we get to choose."

Ella defines a *Should* as how other people want us to live our lives. This is the expectations that others lay upon us. Sometimes a *Should* is light in its weight and can be easily accommodated. At other times the *Shoulds* are highly influential and we feel the pressure to conform and live our lives that is not truly authentic to who we really, really are at the deepest of levels. She goes on to say that when we live in the area of *Should* we are really living our lives for someone or something other than ourselves.

Then there is the *Must*. The *Must* is much different.

"A *Must* is who we are, what we believe, and what we do when we are alone with our truest, must authentic self. It is what calls to us most deeply. Choosing *Must* is the greatest of things we could choose for our lives."

Joe chose his *Must*.

Joe and his wife, Michele own a gym in our local community. If you are a gym rat you are most likely familiar with Cross Fit©. Cross Fit© is the type of gym that Joe and Michele not only own, but founded. I do not know all of the juicy details of Joe's past, but he has eluded to some. I smiled as he told gave out hints about his shenanigans. I smiled because I was remembering my own colorful past and could relate on a level that most people may not understand. I do know Joe finished a Graduate program in Clinical Social Work from a prestigious institution. I do know that after graduating he started working in a nice secure job that allowed him and his family to live a comfortable life with all the bells and whistles that go along with such comforts.

I also know that this was not what Joe wanted deep in his soul. Each day he had a nagging feeling that something was amiss. Yet unable to pinpoint the root cause. Have you ever felt that way; felt something definitely wrong but its origin eluded you? When asked to describe what exactly was, wrong you were unable. Not unwilling to answer, just unable. There is a big difference between the two.

Shortly after graduation, working at his secure job, Joe decided to take action on that feeling. He knew he needed to be true to his own soul, or life would eventually take on a dull sense of underlying regret with the words written on his tomb stone, "If only..............".

In the spring of 2013 Joe and Michele decided to open up a Cross Fit© gym in a very small, rural community located in the heart of Michigan's farm land. The risk was high. The rewards were uncertain. Most people told them it could not possibly succeed and was doomed to failure before it began. Both Joe and Michelle kept their day jobs, but not for long. Realizing that if this business venture was going to have any chance of success, it had to be treated like a business, not a hobby. So, they jumped in with both feet. The result has been a huge success and an embrace from the community; primarily the athletic community. The motto at Cross Fit© is to build not only physical endurance, but mental endurance as well.

My interview with Joe was centered in the arena of fear and how we let fear keep us trapped in our own self-made prison only to realize it is only an illusion we have created. A few months prior to our interview I had conducted a survey of 100 successful adults, asking one question; "What is the number one obstacle that keeps people from getting what they really want out of life?" The results were astounding.

Before I conducted this very short interview with the people I had chosen, I assumed what their answers would be. I imagined that people would blame outside circumstances on their inability to move forward; citing things such as, money, location, kids, spouse, age, resources, and a host of other variable they saw as beyond their control. However, the results indicated something much difference than I had expected. The number one obstacle that 95 out of the 100 people I surveyed stated was fear. A close second and third were self-doubt and limiting self-beliefs, respectively.

Joe shared with me during the interview that this was a *calling* to him. It was more than a business or a gym, it was his mission in life. Hence the title of his business, Mission 1 Cross Fit©. When I asked Joe about fear and if he experienced it, he laughed and responded with, "Every day! In the first year I had to fight the fear off every single minute of every single day. It was really hard. I was afraid I wasn't going to make it, afraid that I wouldn't be able to feed my family or keep a roof over their heads."

Then I asked Joe how the fear was now and he told me it was still there. It never really goes away, we just learn to be friends with it. Respect the fear, but never allow it take the lead. Courage needs to be the leader. Because Joe and Michele are both Christians, they believe that God is their ultimate provider and if this is His vision He will provide the provision. You and I must believe that no matter what. Even if your circumstances are not producing on the outside what you have seen in your heart or hear God speak to you in the quite of the night, we must hold tightly to the truth and promise of that statement.

"It's amazing how God keeps providing for us when we take those steps of faith." Joe said smiling with a deep sense of confidence in his voice and demeanor.

After the interview was over and I was driving home I was reflecting on all that Joe and I had discussed. When I listen to the stories of people who have taken bold steps towards their *Must* in life, I am energized and elated. I always learn something new and take away a new perspective. I was comforted knowing that even those that we perceive as having it all together still experience fear. It never goes away. It is forever within the deep corners of our thoughts waiting for an opportunity to sabotage the vision.

You and I are meant to live a victorious life. A life full of abundance. Abundance does not mean a life free from obstacles and challenges. Those are the very things that keep us laser focused and sharp when we need to move with agility. Raise the sword of your vision. Be a warrior. You need to be ever vigilant and fight for the *Must* in your life. Joan of Arc's response to extreme adversity was, "I am not afraid! I was born to do this!" Joan of Arc died as a warrior at the age of 19 years old. She began her *Must* at the tender age of 16 years old. A young woman fighting during Mid-Evil times against men who had, nor showed mercy. Her final demise was being burned at the stake while the people watched. Rather than forfeit her *Must,* she chose death.

Fortunately for us, the possibility of being burned at the stake is slim and next to none. Yet the stakes are high. The stakes are your very life. You only get one life here on earth. Are you here to survive? I doubt it, or you would not have read this far. You my friend are ready to start thriving. What is your *Must*?

Consider the words of Abraham Maslow, Psychologist, "A musician must make music, an artist must paint, a poet must write, if he is to be ultimately at peace with himself. What a man can be he must be." (Luna. 2015. P. 78-79).

You Can Do This

My youngest daughter, Zoe is a vibrant, intelligent and dynamic 17 year old young woman. As my baby, I tend to be very protective of her. I am not sure if it is because she is the youngest and last child that will be leaving the nest, or that she has always been quiet and introverted. As an extrovert I may feel the need to protect her from the harshness of the outside world.

When she was in 5th grade, Zoe spent a period of time ostracized from a group of her female peers. How long exactly, I am unsure. I only became aware of this when I went to have lunch with her and realized she was sitting by herself in the lunchroom. The other girls has gathered at a nearby table and giggled and laughed in merriment as they ate their lunches. There were some awkward glances Zoe's way from some of the girls as she ate her peanut butter and jelly sandwich, but Zoe appeared not to notice or not to care. As I sat there with my 11 year old daughter, my heart broke. When I asked her why she was sitting alone, she responded with a shrug and a look that told me she really did not want to address the question. I respected her decision and the conversation moved in another direction.

It has been seven years since that day and Zoe is now a junior in high school who enjoys her independence from the social constraints that so often hold an adolescent hostage. She is the type of person who is comfortable to be alone and in many instances, prefers it. Her decisions are not dependent upon another's opinion of what she should or should not do. When she makes up her mind to follow through, there are very few obstacles that stand in her way. I admire those qualities about my baby girl. I admire them a great deal. I sometimes wonder if the challenges she faced in those formative years influenced her personality today. If I were so unaware of what was happening during that time in 5th grade, what are other challenges that my young daughter faced that I was unaware of? It is true that our early experiences shape who we are today. We cannot control what happens to us, but we can control the way we ultimately react to what happens. Taking responsibility for our reactions rather than another's actions or circumstances outside of our control is what provides the fuel of momentum that propels us towards success. If we are wise, we will release anger, guilt and resentment. These three emotions only serve as heavy chains holding us in a dark pit that is far beneath our truest potential and capability.

I use this example of the lunchroom with my daughter, but isn't it true that we can all relate to a time or instance that we felt ostracized at one time or another. Hurt by a painful word, a disapproving glance or the loss of a potentially life changing opportunity. None of us is exempt from pain and obstacle. There are many challenges that come into our lives that we cannot control and in some cases didn't even see coming. It is then that we have the decision to make; to hold onto the anger and bitterness, or to let it go and forgive. Forgive the person, the situation or even forgive yourself.

That truly is the key to moving forward. It is the key to giving yourself permission to let go. To let go of all that is holding you back from living and walking in your potential. It is there. All that you need to live a full and complete life is already within you. It may be hidden underneath years of heartbreak and disappointment. You may even be hesitant to let go of your painful memories for fear that you will once again be disappointed. I encourage you to have the courage to let it go. To embrace a future that is brighter than your past. A future that is unlimited; unlimited only if you choose it to be. The power is yours and I know you can do this.

Zoe has since moved on from her experience. I even wonder if I mentioned it to her if she could recall the incident as vividly as I still do. She has yet to mention it and has never spoken unkindly about the girls who excluded her that day. I am not sure that she even cares that much. She is an independent fire cracker who has plans of her own and isn't too concerned with what happened in the past. What admirable trait. So independent is she that Zoe will spend 12 months immersed in a culture as a foreign exchange student where she does not know the language, the people or the customs. When I asked her if she is afraid to go, she responds with, "Yes, a little. But I am excited too. How cool to go to a place where I will know no one".

Could it be that those earlier experiences became fuel for her dreams rather than a hindrance? Maybe, just maybe, it was those earlier experiences that were preparing her for the journey of life she is destined to be on. Could the experiences you have had be disguised as obstacles to derail you when in fact they are intended to be used as stepping stones to a great opportunity? You may never know. One thing is for sure though, you can make them whatever you want them to be. You can do this. You can turn everything around with your perception. It will take time and a lot of effort but it is so worth it. You're worth it. Your life is worth it.

Take Action:

1. **Listen for your personal *Must***
   If you feel that you need to move forward, move forward. If it is baby steps, so be it. But take them. If you do not you will sit in the seat of "shudda" for the rest of your life. So often we can become

overwhelmed with all there is to do or accomplish. I believe that for many people it is difficult to keep up with the day to day duties of life let alone focus on a compelling vision. It is in those times we need to relax and spend time with our thoughts.

Devote just fifteen minutes a day for sitting alone in a quiet place to just think about your future. Begin to imagine what your future can look and feel like if you had what you desired. Enjoy the moments and let them be just your uninterrupted time. It is during these times that you will become aware of the promptings and subtle ques that God gives you to take a step in a particular direction. Act on what you hear and feel. Make that call. Write that email. Send that note. Apply for that job. When we overthink a decision we may be prompted to put it off. I am not saying to avoid a plan and a strategy! I am simply suggesting that you learn to be obedient in the moment. By learning to take action right away when you need to make bigger decisions that have greater consequences the steps will be easier.

_____

_____

_____

_____

_____

_____

2. **Lean into the awkwardness.**
    It is good for you. Yes, it is very uncomfortable yet if you slowly get used to the feeling you begin to become comfortable with it. It is in these moments that your comfort zone becomes stretched and you are able to handle more and more discomfort. We tend to yield so quickly. Not realizing that if we held on for just a few moments longer and held our ground we may have begun to see the light of hope. Far too many of us run hard and fast away from the discomfort. Thinking that by avoiding it, it will somehow go away. By facing what we feel to be discomfort (I am referring to the healthy kind) we begin to work our courage muscle and it begins to grow stronger and stronger. Start small in the beginning. Maybe you are a very shy person and striking up a conversation with someone you do not know or do not know well is a challenge for

you. Start by deciding to talk with one person a day who you do not know well or you do not know at all. I play this game with myself all the time. For example, when I am grocery shopping I will often challenge myself to say one very sincere compliment to one person I do not know and ask a powerful question to another. I admit, that is a tall order. That simple exercise has been very powerful for me. It has forced me to step outside of my comfort zone and I realize that people appreciate a great compliment and even more they appreciate a good question. How often do we take the time to really ask a deep question? Not very often.

_____

_____

_____

_____

_____

_____

3. **Know your "Why" and make sure it is bigger than your "but"**.
    Knowing your why is singly the most important factor. What I mean is that knowing why you are doing what you are doing will always trump your "but"; I should do that, but.............I would do that, but...............I am just as good as her/him, but...................... Getting what I am saying? If you hold onto your why, your "buts" will fade away. I said earlier in the book that rather than having a traditional "to-do" list I have a great big sign above my computer that asks me the question each time I sit down to work, "What is Your Mission Today?" For me that represents my "Why" in life. Focus on the bigger picture of your life and you will be amazed at how the smaller details no longer have power of your thoughts. You begin to focus on your purpose and what we focus on will grow. Decide what your "Why" is and begin to structure your day, your week, your months and your years centered around that very theme. You will be amazed at the results.

_____

_____

_____

_____

_____

_____

4. Do it before you are ready.

Let's face it. You will never be 100% ready. Waiting for that perfect moment will always elude you. I know this. I lived this. It is not pretty and not comfortable. Even though it gives us the illusion of comfort. The reality it is, it is a lie. Each day you wait, you are wasting the time that was allotted to you by the Creator. You are here for a purpose. You are here by grand design. Start your life and start today.

Here is the question I hear most often, "Someday I really want to _____" (you can fill in the blank). Why is it someday?

I recently facilitated a Leadership Weekend Retreat for 20 dynamic people. When I was first presented with the opportunity I was going to turn it down. It was on very short notice and I was very unfamiliar with the material. I thought to myself, "There is no way I can do this nor do I want to do this!" But, I said yes! Scared crazy, I still said yes. I wasn't ready at the time I was asked, but amazingly I got ready. The weekend was a huge success. I developed valuable relationships that may lead to other opportunities. I did not *feel* ready to take on that venture. It was way outside of my comfort zone. I decided to stretch and give a try. I started before I was ready. Even though it turned out great for me, there have been times things did not turn out as planned. And, that is just fine. I welcome those opportunities because they provide strength and navigation for the future. Never worry about failing. Failing is a part of the process; a very important part of the process. Decide right now to start before you are ready. Write down one thing today that you can start. And, start it. Today.

_____

_____

_____

_____

_____

_____

A New Beginning for You

I truly consider it a privilege to have walked with you on this journey towards claiming a life of thriving and letting go of the survival mentality. I am confident of this: our paths have crossed for a purpose – and that purpose is that you will find the courage to step into all that God has planned for you.

It is my prayer for you that you always remember how special you are in God's eyes. You have so much talent, a multitude of gifts, and a lifetime of experience and passion that has been placed inside of you for a purpose. Avoid minimizing this in your life and settling for a life of survival when you have been created to thrive. Stop "playing small" in your life. It is time for you to have the courage to step into all that God has for you—step up into a higher level. I believe it is in you. I believe that you can accomplish more than you ever dreamed possible. I believe that you can be more and do more than you even realize right now. Never limit yourself. When you limit yourself you are limiting the Power that is within you; you are limiting God. He wants more for you. He has more for you. I am here to support you in any way that I can. You can reach out to me at julie@coachjuliecarr.com or visit my website at www.coachjuliecarr.com for more resources to help you thrive.